TECHNOLOGY AND COMPETITIVENESS IN MEXICO

An Industrial Perspective

Thomas J. Botzman

University Press of America,® Inc.
Lanham • New York • Oxford

Copyright © 1999 by
University Press of America,® Inc.
4720 Boston Way
Lanham, Maryland 20706

12 Hid's Copse Rd.
Cumnor Hill, Oxford OX2 9JJ

Library of Congress Cataloging-in-Publication Data

Botzman, Thomas J.
Technology and competitiveness in Mexico : an industrial
perspective / Thomas J. Botzman.
p.   cm.
Includes bibliographical references and index.
1. Research, Industrial—Mexico. 2. Technology and state—Mexico.
3. Industrial policy—Mexico. I. Title.
T177.M4B68   1999 338.97206—dc21   99—18473 CIP

ISBN 0-7618-1371-3 (cloth: alk. ppr.)
ISBN 0-7618-1372-1 (pbk: alk. ppr.)

⊖™ The paper used in this publication meets the minimum
requirements of American National Standard for Information
Sciences—Permanence of Paper for Printed Library Materials,
ANSI Z39.48—1984

Contents

List of Tables

List of Figures

Preface

With the signing of international trade agreements and the opening of numerous closed economies to international markets, many developing nations are striving to find a competitive edge in the international market. Mexico, in particular, is looking for ways to successfully make the transformation from Third World to First World economic status. This transformation during the past decade has substantially changed the economy from an import substitution model to an open market neoliberal model. Unfortunately, the process has been difficult and unsteady, with the Mexican economy suffering deep recessions and devaluations in 1982, 1994, and 1998.

A large volume of recent literature has pointed to technology transfer practices and industrial transformation as routes to international competitiveness through the growth of a modern manufacturing sector, a key to sustainable economic growth and development. This literature is not only voluminous, but continues to grow in an interdisciplinary fashion (see, for example, Sagafi-nejad, 1991). This book is aimed primarily for industry practitioners looking for a greater understanding of Mexican industrial technology, with a goal of implementing strategies which will succeed as the economic system changes. This book is also intended to be a source of interdisciplinary information for academic researchers, international development organization officials and staff, and government officials interested in the evolving pattern of modern Mexican industrial development. In particular, this book is an attempt to consolidate the growing body of scholarly literature on Mexican technological development, including that published since the foreign reserve crisis and subsequent devaluation of the peso in 1994. The book relies heavily on published literature in assessing the current roles of academia and government in the support of economic development of the industrial sector. It also attempts to provide an objective perspective on the state of industrial development in Mexico, highlighting both strengths and weaknesses. Clearly, this attempt at an objective perspective is difficult when writing from across a national border in a rapidly changing and dynamic environment. In every instance, I have attempted to collect and present data and viewpoints from a variety of aspects in an effort to improve the accuracy of the contents of this book.

This book also hopes to add to the somewhat limited literature on the role of industry in the development process in Mexico, for example, through a deeper inquiry into the role of research, development, and training. The vast majority of earlier literature focuses on the role of government or academia. This is not entirely surprising in light of the critical role of the Mexican government in shaping technology policy during the import-substitution regime. This book seeks to provide a benchmark for the study of modern technology development and competitiveness of Mexican industry. Further, the book attempts to provide a greater understanding of the cooperative linkages that need to be formed between academia, government, and private industry. The case studies of the automobile, textile, chemical, and steel industries are used to illustrate the different forms of industrial structure in Mexico. From these studies, insights may be formed to guide policy and practice toward industrial development for academia, government, and industry.

The author wishes to thank the following for their guidance, counsel and support in the writing of this book: Gaspar Sanchez-Sanchez Mejorada, Javier Cervantes Aldana, Gregorio Herrera Santiago, Anselmo Chavez Capo, Maria Eugenia del Rio Escobar, Maria del Carmen Montes Lora, all of Universidad de las Americas, A.C. in Mexico City; Marco Polo Tello Velasco, Universidad Popular Autonoma del Estado de Puebla; Jose Luis Lopez of ITESM - Estado de Mexico; Gabriela Nava Molina, Universidad LaSalle; Vivian Antaki and Linda Goff of the U.S.-Mexico Commission for Educational and Cultural Exchange, Mexico City; Tagi Sagafi-nejad, Loyola College in Maryland; Robert Mason and Asim Erdilek, Case Western Reserve University; Donald Daly, York University; Harold Williams, Kent State University; Martin Horning, Allison Roberts, Marie Luck, David Zoky, Frank Triplett, Michael Myler, Marty CashBurless, Michelle Collins-Sibley, John Strefeler, Jim Kadlecek, Jim Perone, Harold Kolenbrander, Carol Canavan, Cheryl Paine, Katie Taylor, Bob Sterling, Virgil Brown, Jack DeSario, Saundra Tracy, Mary Ellen

Lloyd, Bob Garland, Bill Howell, Patricia Matthews, Mount Union College; my parents, George and Wilberta Botzman; my family, George and Cindy Botzman, Andy and Carol Botzman, Bill and Virginia Johnson, Bert Botzman, Marlene Botzman, Chris Botzman, Larry and Jane Ann Botzman, John and Lily Botzman, Paul and Michelle Botzman, Mary and John Dabrowsky, Regina and Mike Loss, and Mike Botzman; and my friends, Dave Lemoine, Lawson Wideman, Tony Lauglaug, Rosa and Rollie Rangel-Willequer, Tony Sanor, Bruce Schaefer, Gabriel Bernabeo, Angela Bell, Dane Parker, Anne Zimmer, Tom Spear, Bob Hall, Ron and Kathy Schieber, Rich and Doreen Kuster, Fina Pecchia, Dave Smeltzer, Doug Lowe, Chris Cook, Laura Fish, Joel and Paige Beard, Jim and Donna Benzing, Victoria Mirakian, Bill and Kris Stroud, Barbara Goldstein, Jerry Orosz, Bob and Karen Armbruster, Karen Barnhart, Henry, Beth, and Alyssa Miles, Bettina McNatt, Harry and Ruthanna Wise, and David Crain; the Fulbright-Garcia Robles program; Ciencia Ergo Sum; The Universidad Anahuac del Sur; The North American Economics and Finance Association; the American Society for Competitiveness; the Instituto Nacional de Estadistica, Geografica e Informatica; and the Asociación Nacional de la Industria Química.

I also wish to thank my wife, Vanessa, and my daughter, Gabriela, for their unending love, patience, and support.

The views expressed in this book are those of the author and should not be ascribed to the persons, institutions, or organizations whose assistance is acknowledged. Any remaining errors or omissions are the responsibility of the author.

Thomas J. Botzman
January 1999
North Canton, Ohio

Chapter 1

Introduction

A rapidly modernizing Mexico appeared ready to enter the global marketplace as a major player following the signing of the North American Free Trade Agreement, or NAFTA. However, by the end of 1994, the dream seemed to have been shattered by the economic crisis related to the peso devaluation. In light of the wide swings in Mexican economic performance over the past several decades many questions need to be asked, many of which are related to the use of technology in the industrial sector. When an economy such as Mexico's moves from an internal protected market to one of free trade, what type of institutions and scientific and technological policies emerged during the industrialization, and how did they influence the innovative dynamics of the country? What is the nature of the changes in scientific and technological policies and the institutions that took place as a result of the change toward a free trade regime? (Aboites, 1994). Further, what challenges and threats face the larger businesses and parastatal enterprises as compared to the micro, small, and medium businesses? What roles should be played by government, higher education, and industry in support of sustainable economic growth through effective allocation of research and development resources? How can Mexico achieve higher rates of growth through technological development without disrupting the social and cultural fabric of the country?

Many academics have consumed a considerable amount of time examining the role of Mexico's relatively inexpensive labor in diverting production from the United States and Canada to Mexico. These studies often relate the problems with the labor supply and other production factors, such as the relative scarcity of capital goods, to the difficulties seen in obtaining sustainable economic development in Mexico. Although these areas are problematic, they do not appear to explain all of the difficulties facing Mexico in the global market. Indeed, Mexican workers in 1990 provided $16.30 of value added per hour of labor. Although lower than the United States labor productivity of $23.70 per hour, Mexican labor productivity ranks higher than that of many other nations (OECD, 1994).

Others, however, have attributed the problems of the Mexican industrialization process not to scarcity of production factors, but to problems in acquiring and managing technology as a result of deficiencies in education and personnel training (Patel, 1993). Mexican technology capability is not only lagging that of leading countries, such as the United States, but also is inferior to that of other emerging economies, such as Brazil (Lall, 1992). Economic theory points to technology as a basis of industrialization and economic development. For example, Ricardian trade theory, based on differences in labor productivity among nations, indicates that comparative advantage can be based upon technology leadership. Further, product life cycle theory indicates that the home market can influence innovation through a dynamic process. Nonetheless, the theories do not provide answers as to why certain nations become more competitive, or identify in which industries they will dominate (Porter, 1990). That Mexico has not become internationally competitive in several manufacturing sectors indicates that it has not developed a national infrastructure as is required to support industrial innovation, nor has Mexico sufficiently benefited from efforts to modernize the economy through science and technology programs.

In his comprehensive study on international competitiveness, Porter suggests four factors that determine what firms and what nations will receive financial benefits from innovation: factor conditions, including levels of skilled labor and infrastructure; demand conditions; the existence of strong supporting industries; and firm strategy, structure, and rivalry. The interaction between these factors creates the competitive diamond. According to Porter, a new theory of international competitive advantage must include segmented markets, differentiated products, technology differences, economies of scale, quality, product features, and new product innovation. The central element of the new theory is improvement and innovation in methods and technology, providing managers with insights into the setting of strategy for becoming more effective in the international market (Porter, 1990).

Competitive advantage can be viewed as the advantages present in one firm's value chain over the value chain in another firm. As such, comparative advantage addresses national cost advantages available to an industry, while competitive advantage springs from advantages within the firm which lower costs or improve quality as compared to other producers (Golden, 1994). Comparative advantage may be present in several sectors, while competitive advantage occurs within one sector. In many ways, the evolution of multinational corporations has reduced the importance of comparative advantage based on static factors such as labor costs and national resource endowments. The dynamic factors embodied in the structure of a corporation, including technology capacity and capability, now present the critical competitive advantages which determine which firms will dominate an industry.

According to Golden, competitive advantage has assumed a hierarchical form, with low labor or raw-material cost at the bottom of the competitive scale. These factors, which form the basis of the traditional comparative advantage, were used by many to justify the import substitution strategy in Mexico. In a world without mobility in the factor markets and with a relatively large home market, this strategy was plausible. The modern corporation, however, does not function in a static world divided by national boundaries. The success or failure of a firm is now highly connected to dynamic factors, which are increasing in importance. For example, scale and scope economies are critical to the development of competitive advantage in many industries. The highest levels of competitive advantage result from access to technology, brand names, customer relationships, and cost to customers of changing suppliers. The key insight for strategic planning at the national or firm level is to recognize that the most important factors are created by the firm, not simply arising from the geography of the nation or the historical worker output. Dynamic forces embodied in the firm are more important to sustainable competitiveness than are the traditional static advantages tied to natural resource endowment (Golden, 1994). Relatively abundant oil supplies, or inexpensive labor, are not likely to provide a basis for sustainable competitiveness. If one wishes to create a new strategy, the first step is to examine the present structure of the key players. Consequently, this book seeks to examine the present state of industrial competitiveness in Mexico. Further, it seeks to serve as a benchmark for continued improvement in the assessment of Mexican technological process in the industrial sectors.

Changes in technology and production methods typically require a plan for restructuring of the industrial sector. Industrial restructuring can indicate either a change in the mix of manufactured products between different sectors, or it can indicate the modernization of firms through adoption of new technology, improved organization of production, expanded output, or improvement of product quality (UNCTC, 1992). In this book, the focus is on the latter case. It is increasingly apparent that for Mexico, the keys to sustainable international competitiveness are found in quality, innovation, and manufacturing excellence, and not simply in low wage labor and an artificially low exchange rate. Further, it is clear that adoption of new technology improves the ability of a nation to compete successfully in export markets. Recent decades have seen a notable shift in the composition of global exports by level of technology. Low-technology exports have fallen from forty-five percent of all manufacturing exports during the 1960s to about thirty-five percent today. High technology exports, on the other hand, have risen from 16 to 32 percent of all manufacturing exports (Ostry and Nelson, 1995). Mexican high technology exports are nearly double those for Argentina and Brazil, and are only slightly less than those of Korea (World Bank, 1998).

Nonetheless, innovation and technological change can be important to both low technology and high technology firms if it affects competitive advantage and industry structure (Porter, 1985). A clear implication is that Mexico has much to gain not only by trying to develop industries or firms which lead in a given technology, but also has even more to gain by rapidly infusing technology into the everyday operations of relatively low technology firms (OECD, 1996). Industries which are critical to national economic goals, such as the key role of the apparel industry in maintaining rural employment, then are every bit as important in the development of a technology base as are the high profile, high technology industries.

Linkages between the various strategic sectors improve the efficiency and effectiveness of introducing technological change. As global industry moves toward a fifth generation innovation process[1], it will be increasingly important for businesses to create linkages that include small and large firms, government, and universities (Rothwell, 1994). The development of technology linkages in Mexico, then, is of the highest importance if Mexico is to achieve a competitive posture in global markets. However, the development of technology linkages has been slow and uneven in Mexico, as it has been in many of the other developing economies. The traditional model of Mexican vertical linkages has been the control of a value chain from the earliest stages of the industrial process through to the consumer market. For example, the oil industry in Mexico has, until recently, controlled each step of the industry from oil exploration to the sale of gasoline at Petroleos Mexicanos, or Pemex, stations. The vertical integration was complete and impenetrable by outside competitors, either domestically or internationally. Other industries achieved similar structures without government mandate. The textile industry, for example, is highly vertically integrated from the initially spinning of yarn through the dyeing and finishing processes up to the shipment to apparel firms.

Some authors have indicated that the trend toward vertical integration is subsiding, and that more firms in Mexico are following a route of diversification in becoming less specialized and reducing dependence on costly intermediate product inputs (Siggel, 1996). It is interesting to note that the traditional view that linkages between a firm's value chain and the value chain of suppliers and channels in Mexico has typically taken the form of ownership. The change toward horizontal integration opens the possibility for other innovative forms of cooperation through vertical linkages without ownership control (Porter, 1985). It is exactly these forms of cooperative linkages that are needed to present opportunities for greater industrial competitiveness.

Government, industry, and academia must actively seek to create these linkages, recognizing that the new technology policy and practices must be appropriate for Mexico. The restricted resource base requires that nationalistic pride does not divert funding to industrial sectors where Mexico is not likely to be able to compete, such as the computer hardware industry (Aguilar, 1995). Further, the new policy must continue to reflect competitive realities, reducing government involvement in the sectors which require access to a wider technology and capital market. The petrochemical sector, including the polymer industry, is an example of an area which is likely to become much stronger and more internationally competitive with increasing market competition.

Part of Mexico's problem can also be attributed to the lack of financial resources in support of technology development and transfer, particularly resources derived from inside the country. In fact, Mexico's gross domestic investment as a percentage of GDP has fallen from 27 percent in 1980 to only 15 percent in 1997 (World Bank, 1998). The leading industrial countries have a larger base from which funds can be drawn to support research and development activities. Smaller countries, such as Mexico, typically have far less of a resource base and must develop and use a national system of innovation to focus research and development activities (Hagedoorn and Narula, 1994). Noting that the window of opportunity and public resources available for Mexico are more restrictive than those of the major industrial nations, difficulties in establishing and following a cohesive policy are expected. Mexico, in developing new strategies for science and technology policy, must seek to identify and correct those difficulties and problems.

As noted in a recent OECD study, an effective science and technology program will need to focus on the industrial sector. Such a change will likely meet resistance at both the cultural level from the university and governmental researchers, and at the operational level with businesses unable to determine their exact needs (OECD, 1994). Cultural resistance is also likely to be strong from many of the smaller firms, which are strongly tied to the family structure. Nonetheless, it is apparent that Mexico must make every effort to develop a sustainable science and technology policy. According to Porter, "Firms, not nations, compete in international markets." As such, an understanding of competition must focus on the role of the firm (Porter, 1990). Although government and academia play a key role in the support and formation of a competitive industrial sector, the final analysis must focus on the strengths, weaknesses, and capabilities of firms. This book surveys the roles of science and technology policy in Mexico, including the role of large and small business, the government, higher education, and business training programs. It differs from most previous studies where the focus was on government policy, seeking to highlight the leadership role that needs to be taken by leading industrial sectors. This difference logically follows the shift from government led import substitution policy to an export driven policy.

The leading industrial sectors have become increasingly important to the sustainable development of the Mexican economy. Manufacturing share of GDP has risen rapidly from only 15 percent in 1980 to 23 percent by 1997 (World Bank, 1998). During the decade from 1982 to 1992 manufactures replaced oil as Mexico's primary export, rising from 24 percent to 77 percent of all exports (OECD, 1994). Manufacturing exports from Mexico grew by an average of 16.95 percent from 1987 to 1994, with non-maquiladora exports growing 13.83 percent annually.[2] This contrasts with an overall growth rate for exports of 11.95 percent, including negative growth for industries that enjoy "comparative advantage", such as petroleum and mining products. Imports, however, grew at an even faster rate, averaging 22.83 percent growth between 1987 and 1994. Consumer goods grew at a 43.27 percent annual rate, far outpacing the 26.08 percent in capital goods (OECD, 1996). The growth in consumer goods imports, in particular, was a signal that much of the market growth was not invested in transforming the industrial structure.

Several key industries dominate the growth of manufactured exports. The transportation equipment sector is by far the largest player in the export growth process, followed distantly by metal and machinery, chemicals and petrochemicals, and steel. Those sectors, nonetheless, appear to be increasing in importance to the future growth and stability of the Mexican economy. For example, exports of plastic materials, fibers, and polyvinyl chloride rose ten-fold during the 1980s. Recently, growth of exports has been concentrated in industries with high technology and economies of scale, such as the automobile industry, or in industries characterized by natural resource advantages, such as secondary petrochemicals and steel (UNCTC, 1992). To illustrate the various strategies and programs currently in place, case studies are presented of four important manufacturing sectors: textiles, chemicals (focusing on the production of plastics), metals (focusing on the production of steel), and automobiles.

Throughout this book, balance and objectivity are sought through a broad review of the research literature and available government data. For example, many references will be made to the results of a Mexican government survey, "Encuesta Nacional de Empleo Salarios Tecnologica y Capacitation en el Sector Manufacturero 1992," by the Secretaría del Trabajo y Previsión Social, or STPS, and Instituto Nacional de Estadística, Geografía e Informática, or INEGI. This study, published in 1995, provides the statistical basis for examining the present structure of industrial employment, compensation, technology, and training programs in Mexico. For the purposes of this paper, the "industrial base" has been defined as the textile, petrochemical, metals, and automobile industries.[3] This alternate definition was used to avoid confusion and distortions in the statistics resulting from the large number of micro (less than fifteen employees) food producers in the original STPS and INEGI study. In addition, the new data base avoids complications from the inclusion of the Mexican state oil production industry, Petroleos Mexicanos, commonly known as Pemex. Many of the referenced studies also exclude data from Pemex.

The textile, petrochemical, metals, and automobile industries provide a substantial portion of Mexico's Gross Domestic Product, or GDP, manufacturing base, and employment. It has concerned both government and industry that employment in the manufacturing industries has been falling in several sectors. For example, the textile sector experienced a -4.8 percent annual growth rate in employment from 1987 to 1994, and the basic metal industry lost 7 percent of all jobs during the same period. The metal industry downsizing is largely a result of improved technology and rationalization of production. The textile industry, on the other hand, employs less workers largely as a result of inability to compete with foreign producers (OECD, 1996).

In addition, each sector plays an important role in the potential development of the Mexican economy through linkages into other sectors and has been a leading player in the importation of foreign technology (Pfaff et al, 1993). The textile industry is a major employer of women and unskilled workers, and a leading export sector. It also provides employment in rural areas away from the industrial centers. The petrochemical sector absorbs production of raw materials from the state-owned oil and gas production plants and is a major employer in the Gulf Coast region. The metals sector provides intermediate materials for use in many of the other manufacturing sectors, and has also been growing rapidly in export capacity. The diverse locations of the steel mills provide employment in several areas of the country, particularly in Monterrey and Puebla. The automobile sector provides many of the backward vertical linkages into the rest of the industrial base, and is a likely sector for the creation of jobs in Mexico. It provides a high level of employment in the north of the country. The four identified sectors clearly provide linkages into many other industrial sectors and represent a geographical cross-section of the manufacturing industry in Mexico. Profiles of the four industries are provided in TABLE 1.1 below.

TABLE 1.1

ECONOMIC PROFILES FOR THE TEXTILE, CHEMICAL,
METALS, AND AUTOMOTIVE SECTORS, 1993

	Percent National GNP	Percent National Workers	Percent Manuf. GNP	Percent Manuf. Workers
Textiles	2.2	1.6	9.4	15.0
Chemicals	3.7	1.2	16.3	11.8
Metals	1.0	0.2	4.3	1.8
Automobile	2.9	0.8	12.5	7.6

Source: INEGI, 1995

The four selected sectors provide different aspects from which to view the need, sourcing, and prospects for technology development in Mexican industry. The textile and apparel sector is an example of a "supplier-dominated sector" in the development of products and processes. Changes in capital goods and intermediate inputs, such as synthetic fibers, have driven the exploitation of opportunities for new textile and clothing products. The automotive and metals sectors, on the other hand, are examples of "scale-intensive sectors" in which size plays a leading role in guiding complex process and product development. These sectors also tend to vertically integrate to take advantage of both forward and backward linkages. The petrochemical sector is an example of a "science-based sector," relying heavily on product and process innovation to create new capital or intermediate inputs. Formalized research and capital intensive production processes characterize the science-based industries (Dosi, 1988).

The opening of the economy to international competition has been accompanied by a rapid transfer of industrial and service sectors from state to private control. The reprivatization of the parastatal firms began in 1982, with 776 firms privatized during the following six years. The largest firms, however, were not sold until the Salinas administration took power following the 1988 elections. The number of parastatal firms was reduced from 1,155 in 1982 to 213 by 1993. The Zedillo administration has been completing the privatization effort, selling the national railroads, electric generation plants, ports, and downstream activities of Pemex (OECD, 1996). The value added by parastatal firms has steadily dropped from 6.7 percent of GDP in 1985 to 4.9 percent of GDP by 1995 (World Bank, 1998). Noting that the petroleum industry giant, Pemex, remains in state hands, much of the privatization effort is now complete. It remains to be seen if the future will bring privatization of all or part of Pemex, but for now it appears that Pemex will remain under state ownership and control.

The four selected sectors also represent a range of different levels of past and present government involvement. The textile and apparel sector has been, and remains, largely privately owner. A significant aspect of government involvement in the industry is through the creation of a large number of geographically dispersed maquiladora operations that supply the U.S. market. The petrochemical industry has been one of the most highly protected industries, and continues to be dominated by the parastatal giant Pemex.[4] The downstream products of the petrochemical industry continue to be privatized, with Mexico removing restrictions on 14 of the 19 petrochemical categories and all secondary petrochemicals (OECD, 1996). The steel industry has been largely privatized during the past decade, with the privatization of Sidermex signaling the transfer of the largest steel mill in Mexico into private hands. The steel industry has rapidly moved from parastatal domination to nearly total private Mexican ownership. The automobile industry has been and likely will continue to be private, with most operations falling under the control of multinational corporations based outside Mexico. The unique blend of public and private ownership has a pronounced effect on the ability to raise capital in each sector.

The source of investment capital for the selected sectors is summarized in TABLE 1.2. Obviously, the high level of foreign ownership in the automobile industry provides greater access to both investment and portfolio capital, although direct investment predominates as the multinationals continue to construct and improve auto plants. The metals industry, on the other hand, is challenged to raise international capital and may need to create additional international joint ventures to increase access to capital needed for plant and equipment investments. The likely rise in foreign ownership in most industries will continue to improve the access of various industry sectors to capital and hard currency.

TABLE 1.2

CAPITAL SOURCE FOR SELECTED INDUSTRIES, 1991

	Private National	Parastatal National	Foreign Ownership
Textiles	85.6	3.7	10.7
Chemicals	58.2	13.4	28.3
Metals	79.0	17.2	3.7
Automobile	27.6	0.0	72.4

Source: STPS and INEGI, 1995

The industries also vary by age of the firm. The age of a firm is often used to characterize its maturity in various facets of doing business, such as willingness to take risks on new products or process technology. In many cases the relative youth of firms indicates smaller size. In Mexico, textile firms tend to be younger than those in the other three selected sectors, with metals firms are slightly older than others. Relatively few Mexican firms can be considered old by the traditional industry standards of more developed countries. Age of the firm may indicate a different propensity to adopt new technology, equipment, and training methods that will change the competitive posture of a firm. For example, the newer minimill technology is relatively more prevalent in the Mexican steel industry among younger firms, providing a modern base for export production. The age of firms by sector is summarized in TABLE 1.3.

TABLE 1.3

AGE OF FIRMS IN YEARS FOR SELECTED INDUSTRIES,
PERCENT OF FIRMS, 1991

	0 - 3	4 - 15	16 - 25	26 - 45	46 or more
Textiles	22.8	54.2	8.4	11.9	2.7
Chemicals	7.2	55.8	17.9	15.5	3.6
Metals	6.5	33.1	44.4	13.5	2.6
Automobile	6.9	50.2	20.1	21.4	1.4

Source: STPS and INEGI, 1995

Capacity utilization is another important indicator of past and present industrial competitiveness. Capacity utilization varies with the size of the firm, with the largest firms running at the highest percentage of capacity. The introduction of new technology will not only improve the ability of Mexican firms to export goods, but in many industries will provide firms with the ability to readily fill domestic demand. Recognizing the growth of the Mexican population and personal incomes, growth in manufacturing capacity is likely to be a key concern in many of the industrial sectors. Capacity utilization is summarized in TABLE 1.4.

TABLE 1.4

CAPACITY UTILIZATION FOR SELECTED INDUSTRIES BY
SIZE OF FIRM, 1991

	Large	Medium	Small	Micro
Textiles	80.6	75.6	69.6	74.3
Chemicals	81.6	74.1	72.6	67.5
Metals	81.4	71.7	70.8	71.9
Automobile	88.0	71.7	62.1	77.8

Source: STPS and INEGI, 1995

The automobile industry, in particular, appears to run near capacity as a means of reducing total cost and covering the large plant and equipment investments. The presence of excess capacity also indicates that some sectors of Mexican industry can continue to expand exports without straining the total ability of the plant to produce. This was particularly evident following the devaluation of 1994, when many Mexican producers shifted resources toward the export sector. For example, steel exports to the United States soared during 1995, providing an ability to continue to grow despite the steep downturn in the domestic economy. However, in some cases the lack of suitable inputs or production bottlenecks may prevent fuller use of installed plant and equipment.

---

[1]Models of innovation have been segmented into five periods: the technology-push first generation of the 1950s and early 1960s, the need-pull second generation of the late 1960s, the coupling model third generation of the 1970s, the integrated model fourth generation of the 1980s, and the current systems integration and networking fifth generation. For a more complete discussion, see Rothwell (1994).

[2] Maquiladoras, or in-bond manufacturing plants, manufacture goods destined for export. Although most maquiladoras are located near the US-Mexico border, plants are increasingly located toward the interior of the country. Recent changes have provided increased opportunities to serve the domestic market. The great majority of maquiladoras are under foreign control, primarily by US multinationals.

[3]The industries surveyed include textiles (INEGI 3200; 16,633 firms), chemicals (INEGI 3500; 4,933 firms), metals (INEGI 3700; 884 firms) and automobiles (INEGI 3841, 866 firms). A total of 52 sectors were surveyed. Several of the other sectors were excluded from this study, most notably the food, beverage, and tobacco sector (INEGI 3100; 50,355 firms). It was felt that the more than 47 thousand micro enterprises in the food, beverage, and tobacco sector would distort and compromise the findings of this study. A total of 138,774 firms were surveyed by STPS and INEGI during 1992. The firms were segregated into four groups by size: 2,094 large firms with 251 or more employees; 2,720 medium firms with between 101 and 250 employees; 13,117 small firms with between 16 and 100 employees; and 120,843 micro firms with between 1 and 15 employees. Firms were broadly categorized into the following subsectors: INEGI 31, food, beverages, and tobacco; INEGI 32, textiles and clothing; INEGI 33, wood and wood products; INEGI 34, paper and paper products, printing and publishing; INEGI 35, chemical substances, organic products, rubber, and plastics; INEGI 35, non-metallic mineral products, such as ceramics, glass, and cement; INEGI 37, basic metals; INEGI 38, metal products, machinery, and equipment; and INEGI 39, other manufacturing industries.

[4]Note that the statistics provided by STPS and INEGI do not clearly reflect the dominant role of Pemex in the petrochemical industry.

Chapter 2

An Overview of Mexican R&D and Technology Transfer

The import substitution model of development as it was followed in Mexico retarded the creation of technology rich pockets in the Mexican industrial sector. Many sectors, such as some parts of the apparel industry, operate the same today as they did decades ago, recalling the description of the apparel industry in Mexico as a "backward" industry. Technological backwardness is defined as "insufficient development of the set of social practices through which information is expected to become knowledge applied to production" (Patel, 1993). Some industries in Mexico are likely to be at a substantial competitive disadvantage because of their "technological backwardness" as the economy is opened to increased international competition. Examples from the economic literature include the Mexican automobile, chemical, transport equipment, machinery, and iron and steel industries (Leamer, 1993). Many of the challenges facing these industries can be traced to past, present, and future deficiencies in the application of research, development, and technology transfer programs. Mexican industry, as a result of decades of import-substitution policy, has not had access to the same technology or capital structure as is used by many foreign competitors and multinational corporations (Sterner, 1990). Since domestic producers had little incentive to innovate, a culture that did not value technology leadership was created (Patel, 1993). Eventually, Mexico will not only need to adopt newer technology, but will also need to shape a new attitude toward innovation in order to become competitive in domestic and foreign markets.

Patel defines domestic technological capability as, "The ability to organize the productive process, absorb the external technological advances and use them for the purpose of expanding constantly the technological capacity of a society." He notes that there are many levels of research and development capability required by a firm, including selection of appropriate technology, the search for available technical alternatives, mastery and effective utilization of the technology adapted to the specific production conditions, development of new or improved technologies and know-how through minor innovations, and conducting basic research activities (Patel, 1993). The innovative capability can then be used to produce products that are competitive not only in domestic markets, but also in the international marketplace. As production and distribution follows, the resulting differences in a firm or a nation's productivity and efficiency can then be attributed to differences in technology, age of capital equipment, economies of scale, or plant operating performance (Sterner, 1990). By linking leading-edge innovative capability to effective and efficient production, a firm or nation may establish leadership in a product area. Further, the nation that follows in the adoption of new technology will consistently fall behind those nations that establish technology leadership, losing markets and time while the technology lag is overcome (Porter, 1990).

Mexico can be described as a follower for most of this century. In some sectors Mexico is not only a follower, but unable to effectively implement new or imported technologies. Foreign Direct Investment, or FDI, is critical to a country's ability to receive new technology, especially when the domestic technology base lags behind that of competitor nations. FDI, as an efficient method to transfer technology, may become even more appropriate as advanced technologies are imported which substitute for lagging domestic technologies. Nevertheless, Mexico must select which foreign technology to import so as not to become totally dependent on imported technology (Lall, 1992). Clearly, FDI is one of the most important mechanisms of the productive system in the acquisition of external technological innovations. Given Mexico's proximity to the United States, and the consequent need to compete effectively in the U.S. market, the importance of sustainable FDI is imperative. The need becomes even greater in recognition of the continued trend toward an open-arms era and multilateral cooperation inspired by the World Trade Organization (Sagafi-nejad, 1995).

A litany of arguments are commonly used to create support for the development of greater public encouragement of FDI. Positive arguments in favor of foreign investment flow include obtaining technological patents related to foreign investment make the acquisition of technology easier and spread the new administrative methods; the entrance of foreign enterprises to reinforce the competitive environment in domestic markets, which stimulates technological change; and encouraging the development of finance in the market for risk capital related to technological innovations (Aboites, 1994). Unfortunately, much of the financial flow into Mexico was made as stock portfolio investment with money from mutual funds, leading to the likelihood of rapid withdrawals following negative economic or political news (Lowenthal, 1993).[1] Portfolio investment shifts played a large role in the drain on reserves to support the peso, and consequently contributed to the peso crisis. The impact of foreign direct investment, on the other hand, was relatively small (Gunther et al, 1996). Portfolio investment, in the case of Mexico, does not appear to have significantly contributed to the stability and usefulness of a growing productive capital stock.

As a key part of the neoliberal restructuring of the economy, FDI policy was reformed. The National Development Plan of 1989 to 1994 envisioned four roles for foreign direct investment in Mexico: creation of employment opportunities, new financial resources for indebted firms, acquisition of newer technology, and increasing manufactured product exports (UNCTC, 1992). Many observers assumed that these four goals would be met through the passage of the North American Free Trade Agreement, or NAFTA. Indeed, NAFTA expectations positively influenced the inward flow of foreign investment, through both increased interest in the Mexican market and the trend toward larger Mexican businesses with joint ventures and direct linkages to the U.S. capital markets. This effort, it was hoped, would increase share of FDI aimed at Mexico and Latin America, which currently receives less than one-half the FDI of developing Asian nations (Sagafi-nejad, 1995). The increased FDI was primarily aimed at capital and technology-intensive industries, decreasing commitment to traditional natural resource (i.e. oil industry) and labor-intensive industries (Ostry and Nelson, 1995).

To develop a stable increase in the useful capital stock, Mexico must attract additional foreign direct investment to supplement and complement foreign portfolio investment. Mexico appeared to be reaching that goal during the early 1990s, receiving nearly twenty percent of the total capital inflows to all developing countries. The

1990 legal reform of technology transfer agreement regulations appeared to create a sustainable interest in FDI toward Mexico (Whiting, 1991). Although overshadowed by $28 billion of portfolio investment during 1993, net foreign direct investment reached a high of $16.6 billion (Folkert-Landau and Ito, 1995).   Unfortunately, FDI levels crashed following the peso devaluation of 1994, returning to the very low levels of the mid 1980s. See FIGURE 2.1.   It is now readily apparent that any plan to modernize the technology infrastructure in Mexico will need to be accompanied by consistent support from the Mexican government and the banking community. A key step in this process is to organize an independent central bank which is not used to improve the political fortunes of those in political power.

FIGURE 2.1

FOREIGN DIRECT INVESTMENT IN MEXICO, 1980 - 1997
BILLIONS OF DOLLARS

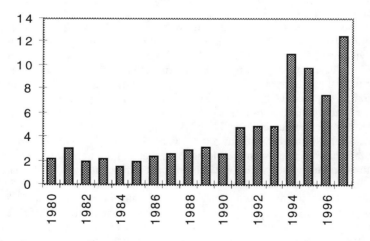

Source: INEGI

    Much of the present foreign direct investment is taking the form of partnerships or equity shares, usually in the form of joint ventures or purchase of Mexican companies. Mexican firms, at times willingly, are seeking out partners to increase their technology capabilities.

Hagedoorn and Narula define technology partnering as "inter-firm cooperation for which a combined innovative technological activity or an exchange of technology is at least part of an agreement." They then divide technology partnering into two categories, interorganizational modes and contractual alliances.   Interorganizational modes require equity sharing, such as the formation of joint ventures or joint research and development organizations.   The more mature industries, such as steel and automobiles, rely more heavily on joint ventures and shared R&D activities.   Contractual alliances, which do not have equity sharing, include joint development agreements, research agreements, licensing, and sourcing agreements.   The high-technology industries, such as biotechnology and software, usually rely on contractual alliances to provide increased research and development flexibility. Joint ventures typically require a new organizational structure and a long time frame for success.   Contractual alliances, on the other hand, are more focused and generally are used for a relatively short period of time (Hagedoorn and Narula, 1994).

Many reasons exist for the formation of technological alliances, including reduction of technological risk, increased access to consumer markets, avoidance of political problems, differences in national rules and licensing statutes, reduced design cost, defense of internal markets, flexibility of production, and creation of investment funding (Molina, 1995).   The long run advantages are potentially even more valuable, because collaboration and competition between firms inside a market segment can provide competitive advantages not just to the leading firm, but also to other firms in the market.   Sustained interactions between suppliers and producers can, over time, increase the level of innovation while lowering its cost (Marceau, 1994).   The greatest advantage of having domestic suppliers is in the innovation and upgrading process. Through cooperative research and development, the firms can reach improved solutions to a wide range of problems.   The suppliers can then spread those solutions to other firms, increasing the speed of technology transfer between domestic firms.   The absence of geographical and cultural distances also makes the linkages between domestic suppliers and manufacturing firms stronger and more effective than those between foreign suppliers and the manufacturing firms.   The innovative culture creates not only changes in technology, but also better methods for doing things.   Evidence of innovation can be found in product and process changes, new approaches to marketing, new forms of distribution, and new conceptions of scope.   Porter notes that innovation at the level of the firm results from increased knowledge and skills, not only through research and development activities but also through organizational learning (Porter, 1990).   In effect, the technology learning curve is shortened by domestic firms working together and learning from each other.

The four sectors presented in the case studies provide an array of positions toward technology partnering. Joint ventures are relatively common in some sectors of the Mexican petrochemical and steel industries, while foreign ownership is prevalent in the Mexican automobile industry.[2] In many cases, the automobile firms have developed a form of quasi-integration across national borders (Contractor, 1986). The textile and apparel industry, on the other hand, is dominated by small firms without joint ventures or foreign ownership. Globally, the number of joint ventures in the area of new materials is uncharacteristically high, most likely as a result of the large number of steel, chemical, and engineering firms entering this field to defend against the replacement of their traditional products. Worldwide, approximately 65 percent of chemical company alliances are joint ventures, followed by the automobile industry with approximately 50 percent joint ventures (Hagedoorn and Narula, 1994).

Although developed countries have a long history of cooperative production through subsidiaries and subcontracting, the phenomenon of industrial linkages between industrial and developing countries is a relatively new phenomenon, growing rapidly since World War II. Data on the amount of production abroad was only gathered beginning during the 1960s, and a lack of clear data continues to complicate the analysis of the type and intensity of cooperative ventures in creation of technology transfer (Grunwald and Flamm, 1985). Most studies of international strategic alliances have been conducted on alliances between developed country firms or institutions, leaving a gap in the study of alliances between developed countries and developing countries. For U.S. firms, approximately thirty-nine percent of all strategic alliances are entirely domestic, with the remaining sixty-one percent international. Of the international alliances, fifty-seven percent were with firms in Japan or Western Europe, and ten percent were with Russian firms. Mexican firms involved in strategic alliances with U.S. firms participate in the finance, telecommunication, construction, and retail industries. Most U.S.-Mexican strategic alliances take the form of joint ventures rather than contractual alliances (Murray, 1995).

The analysis of effective technology transfer practices in a developing nation, then, is often quite complicated. For example, the assessment of the effectiveness of Mexican technology transfer through partnerships is often perplexing in that quite often lists of multinational organizations are used as a surrogate for real technology transfer (Sklair, 1993). Nonetheless, the reported average percentage of income used by the surveyed firms for the purchase or transfer of technology is generally consistent, with most firms spending around three percent of income for technology transfer (STPS and INEGI, 1995). It may be inferred that few firms in Mexico, regardless of size, are able to afford large amounts of technology transfer. Moreover, the percentage of income for purchase of technology or technology transfer is relatively consistent among the key industries surveyed, ranging from a high of 2.6 percent for the textile industry to a low of 2.0 percent for the automobile industry. It is important to note that the relatively small size of the textile firms probably biases the reported percentage upward, and that in any case the level of income expended for technology transfer is quite low. Nonetheless, given the extremely low expenditures for R&D inside the company, technology transfer is likely to remain an important source of relatively new technology. See TABLE 2.1

These spending levels reflect the commonly held belief that a minimal level of R&D is required for successful imitation, as R&D provides a basis for recognizing and selecting external technological advances in addition to direct development of new products. In many countries, the impact of imitation and innovation are combined in product and process development through improvement of a firm's absorptive capability. Although only a few studies have related innovation to variables such as R&D expenditures, patents, and the number of scientists and engineers, those studies that have used these variables have shown a strong positive impact of private R&D on both the level and growth of productivity (Fagerberg, 1994). For Mexico, this indicates that effective technology policy to encourage additional industrial R&D is necessary for improved international competitiveness through a process of continuous innovation.

TABLE 2.1

AVERAGE PERCENT OF INCOME SPENT FOR TECHNOLOGY TRANSFER BY INDUSTRY AND SIZE, 1991

	Total	Large	Medium	Small	Micro
Textiles	3.0	3.4	2.6	2.7	1.5
Chemicals	2.7	2.6	2.0	2.2	6.9
Metals	3.3	3.1	1.9	3.1	6.4
Automobile	2.3	2.2	2.3	4.2	2.3

Source: STPS and INEGI, 1995

Mexican industry has historically relied more heavily on domestic technology than do industries in other emerging economies. More than one-half of the technology purchased by the Mexican firms is supplied by other Mexican firms. Only 15 percent was imported from the United States, followed by Germany at 9 percent. Other countries supplying technology included Italy, Japan, Switzerland, France, Spain, Canada, Great Britain, Sweden, and the Netherlands. Mexico and the United States dominated all four of the selected industries, with Germany supplying a substantial quantity of technology for the automobile industry and Italy and France considerable technology for the textile industry (STPS and INEGI, 1995; Pfaff et al, 1993).

Cultural forces continue to dictate that most of the technology transfer in Mexico will be from domestic sources. In particular, Mexican executives view barriers to technology transfer as originating in the home country as a result of different cultural norms, such as education and work ethic (Dean and Le Master, 1991). In the long run, the domination of Mexican firms in the supply of technology will result in an increasing technology gap as compared to the more industrialized economies, as the technology supplied is likely to be less advanced than that from other nations. Mexican supply of technology prevents using new technology to leapfrog gaps in the current system. Occasionally, imported technology is used to address a deficiency in domestic infrastructure. An example of the leapfrog phenomenon is the way that Mexican firms have jumped over the problem of poor postal service by employing new technologies such as fax and e-mail. Unfortunately, this type of rapid employment of new technology is relatively unlikely to become widespread in the area of manufacturing technology.

Mexico's R&D system is composed of four key players, including government, higher education institutions, industry, and non-profit institutions (OECD, 1994). Under the import substitution model, the government sector was the only sector that functioned to any great degree. Even today, the public sector controls virtually all of the formal research and development activity in Mexico. Of the 4,612 members of the National System of Innovation in 1990, only 32, or 0.7 percent, worked for private sector institutions. Federal institutions under the Secretaría de Educación Pública, or SEP, the Mexican educational ministry, employed 62.4 percent of all investigators. The remaining 36.9 percent were employed by other federal agencies, primarily in the Mexico City area. Three out of every ten researchers in the country works for the Universidad Nacional Autonoma de Mexico, or UNAM, the national university located in Mexico City (Molina, 1995).

The Mexican model of support for research and development, with less than 20 percent of funding originating in the private sector, differs radically from the model employed in the leading industrial nations (OECD, 1994). For example, Japanese industry contributes 76 percent of the total spending for research and development, followed by government at 18 percent and universities at 5 percent. Further, the firms also contribute through "shop floor" innovation activities, effectively raising the role of the private sector. Mexico's eighty percent of funding originating in the government sector also contrasts sharply with a governmental share of research and development funding at about 50 percent for France, 45 percent for the United States, 35 percent in Germany, and 37 percent in the United Kingdom (Fransman, 1994). It should be noted, however, that the share of Mexican private industry investment in R&D has increased during the past decade, growing at an annual rate of over 10 percent (OECD, 1994). Nonetheless, Mexico must continue to work toward comparable levels of private industry support for research and development as is seen in the leading industrial countries. Those areas which provide spillover effects to other industries through creation of technology formal and informal technology linkages are, if identified, favored for government and private sector support. The wide range of possible technological systems also requires that Mexican government and industry address specific problems in each key functional technology area, rather than use a shotgun approach to solving problems (Carlsson, 1994).

Relatively few Mexican firms are actively involved in the conduct of research and development activities, paralleling the practice of most Third World nations. The leading industrial countries conduct more than 90 percent of all R&D studies, leaving little room for leading-edge development in the lesser developed countries. For example, the United States remains the world leader for research and development, with a total greater than the combined research and development of the entire European Community. Eighty percent of United States R&D spending is accounted for by eight industries: aircraft, computer and office equipment, pharmaceuticals, instruments, scientific instruments, motor vehicles, chemicals, and electrical machinery (National Science Board, 1993). Mexico follows the same pattern of concentrated spending in a relatively few sectors, led by the petrochemical, electronics, and telecommunications industries.

Indeed, most Mexican firms appear to have little value carrying out internal research, but are constantly searching for new sources of domestic or foreign technology in an effort to remain competitive in the international market (Rubio, 1984). Of the surveyed firms in the four industries, only 12 percent report having done any R&D investigations since 1989. In all four sectors the number of firms participating in R&D was less than 50 percent, and in the textile industry more than 90 percent of all firms did not participate in any research and development activity. As the industry segments increase the level of joint ventures and foreign direct investment, it can be expected that the level of R&D activity will dramatically rise, eventually approaching the levels experienced in other industrialized countries.

TABLE 2.2

ESTABLISHMENTS CONDUCTING R&D SINCE 1989

	Total	Yes	No	Don't Know
Textiles	16,663	1,969	13,670	1,023
Chemicals	4,933	2,230	2,611	92
Metals	446	297	573	15
Automobile	565	389	465	12

Source: STPS and INEGI, 1995

The burden of providing research and development activities falls more heavily on the firms with fewer employees, especially the micro firms since many of the technology firms in Mexico are relatively young and small. The majority of micro technology-driven firms in Mexico are not aiming for widespread markets, but instead are seeking to better serve niche markets, hoping to exploit speed in gaining a competitive edge (Corona, 1994). Among the firms reporting R&D activity since 1989, the large firms spent roughly one-half the percentage of income for R&D than did the micro firms. The average percentage of income spent for R&D for all sizes of companies was always under one percent, a level considerably lower than the approximately two percent of sales that most industrial firms in developed countries dedicate to research and development activities. In some part, this may be explained in that those plants that are part of multinational firms may be obtaining research and development activity from the parent, reducing the need for spending by the subsidiary. In any event, very little income is being invested in R&D activity inside Mexico. Nonetheless, it is likely that the low level of research and development spending is an artifact of the import-substitution policy, when Mexican firms did not need to spend to compete with imported products. See Figure 2.2.

FIGURE 2.2

AVERAGE PERCENT OF INCOME SPENT FOR R&D
BY SIZE

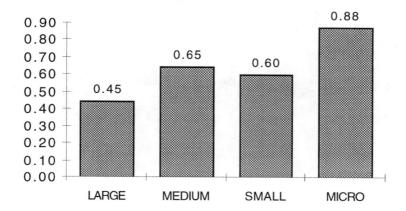

Source: STPS and INEGI, 1995

At the macroeconomic policy level, it is clear that Mexico will continue to need new laws and regulations which encourage growth of research and development spending. For example, the United States encourages research and development through the use of a mix of credits, accelerated depreciation, and tax deductions. South Korea and Taiwan use credits, accelerated depreciation, tax deductions, and patent extensions. Mexico has historically relied solely on tax deductions (Clavijo and Márquez, 1994). Tax breaks and abatements may be required to encourage investment by private industry in new technological capability. Mexico spends approximately 0.33 percent of all gross domestic expenditures on research and development, a level consistent with other developing nations but far short of spending in developed countries.

However, the commitment to research and development funding has been improving in recent years. Mexico's federal spending for science and technology, though modest by international standards, has been rising. In 1988, spending was 0.27 percent of GDP and had reached 0.39 percent by 1993 (Sánchez Ugarte, 1994). In particular, R&D spending by the private sector, at 0.08 percent of gross domestic expenditures, is notably lower than what is expected for a country of Mexico's size and level of development. In contrast, recent spending for research and development totals 2.15 percent of GDP in Japan, 1.81 percent of GDP in the United States, and 1.32 percent of GDP in the European Union (OECD, 1994). The Mexican government is hopeful that expenditures for R&D can rise above one percent of GDP during the next decade. Nonetheless, the gap in resources available for R&D makes current effective and efficient planning even more critical if the Mexican economy is to develop.

---

[1] Some authors reject the linkage between portfolio investment and the peso crisis. See, for example, Folkerts-Landau, 1995.

[2] Sixteen percent of the foreign direct investment through debt for equity swaps of 1986 Brady Plan was directed toward the automotive sector, resulting in substantial investments by Volkswagen, Chrysler, and Nissan (UNCTC, 1992).

Chapter 3

Mexican Technology Transfer History and Development Planning

Economic growth results from changes in population, productivity, or cultural progress. The majority of Mexican economic growth over recent decades has resulted from growth in the population, not from growth in productivity or cultural progress. While population growth averaged about 2 percent per year, the growth in productivity appears to be unsteady at best during the past fifteen years. In some studies, the level of growth of Mexican labor and capital productivity has been reported to be quite low or even negative (see, for example, Anderson, 1993). This is in sharp contrast to economic growth and development in the industrialized nations, which is often attributed to rapid increases in productivity (Patel, 1993).

The growth rate of GDP has increased during the past decade, rising to 1.8 percent growth during to 1990s from 1.1 percent average growth during the 1980s. However, the annual growth rate for value added by industry has fallen from 10.3 percent to 5.5 percent per year during the same time period (World Bank, 1998). Lacking real productivity gains, recent Mexican economic growth has not resulted in sustainable economic development of the manufacturing sector in a manner consistent with other industrialized economies. This is evident in the cyclical changes in Mexican Gross Domestic Product from year to year.

Subtracting the approximately two percent growth in economically active population, many recent years have actually realized negative growth in productivity, indicating that the growth prospects for Mexico have been, and likely will continue to be, somewhat unequal into the next decade. See Figure 3.1.

FIGURE 3.1

ANNUAL CHANGE IN GDP
PERCENT, 1980 - 1997

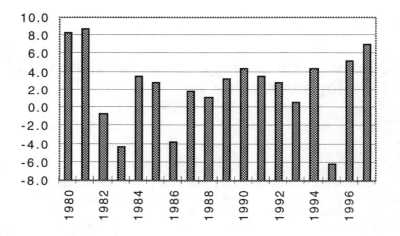

Source: INEGI

Another way of viewing productivity is the relative GDP per employed person. The average Mexican worker is able to produce slightly less than one-half the output value of a Canadian or US worker. About 37 percent of the Mexican population is employed and produces about $7384 in per capita GDP, resulting in a GDP per employed person ratio of $19956. This compares to the Canadian worker's $40488 and the United States worker's $52794 (UNDP, 1997).[1] Although wages remain much lower in Mexico, the output per worker partially offsets that advantage.

A review of Mexican economic policy and performance during this century reveals many of the underpinnings of the relatively low and unsteady growth in productivity. Mexico progressed through three periods of development starting with the industrialization phase beginning in 1930. This period featured nationalization of industry, including most sectors of the petrochemical, electricity, nuclear power, railroad, and telecommunications industries. One of Mexico's most revered historical figures is Lazaro Cardenas, who as president initiated much of the nationalization of industry, particularly the oil. In general, the industrialization phase was able to provide limited growth in many of the important industrial sectors, but was unable to create an economy that was competitive with the leading economies of Europe and the United States.

The presidential election of 1968 signaled the beginning of the second period, which was aimed at stabilizing the gains of the earlier decades. Unfortunately, the import substitution policies of the 1950s and 1960s had led to an external dependence for technology, much of which was acquired from the United States. Since most technology was imported from the United States, Mexico had no policy for national management of technology, little technology was of domestic origin, and absorption of technology was hindered by lack of management and worker skills (Patel, 1993). Although Mexico wanted to modernize the technological infrastructure, there were no central locations available to attract investment and researchers with the skills to develop the new technology. Even when Mexico was able to import or develop technology, the skilled workers were far behind on the learning curve as compared to workers from the more developed nations.

The third period began in 1975, but in reality only began to take hold during the 1980s. Mexico initiated an outward-looking policy aimed at attracting technology, trade, and investment from other countries to supplement domestic development activities. The process has been complicated in that Mexico's protection of domestic industry during the proceeding period created two very different structures of firms. The larger firms tend to produce most of the intermediate, capital, and durable consumer goods, while the smaller firms are left to produce the less sophisticated goods. This split in production has created a wide divide between the technological capabilities of small and large businesses, retarding the development of backward linkages between firms of different sizes. In turn, this has retarded the development of linkages between academic research and industrial technology to be used by small firms (Sobarzo, 1992). The radical economic changes have been accompanied by substantial political and social unrest, in addition to substantial financial hardships as the result of the severe recession of the early 1980s and the peso devaluation of 1994.

The goal of the new government economic planning programs is to turn Mexico's growth into real and sustainable development. According to Sklair, there are six requirements for changing growth into development: linkages through exports and imports, retention of foreign exchange, upgrading of personnel, improved conditions of labor, genuine technology transfer, and a functioning distribution system (Sklair, 1993).   Mexico has consistently been deficient in several of these areas as needed for sustainable economic development.   Linkages between exports and imports in past years were few, with much of the export strategy based on the export of petroleum.   This has changed to an extent, with exports as a percentage of GDP rising from 11 percent in 1980 to 22 percent by 1997.   Further, manufactured exports as a percentage of all merchandise exports rose from 12 percent in 1980 to 78 percent in 1996 (World Bank, 1998).   In addition, the deficit in the current account consistently challenged the ability of the Mexican banking system to retain foreign exchange.   Little was done during the 1980s to upgrade the skills of personnel or to improve the conditions of labor, largely as a result of the hardships imposed by the deep recession. Mexico did little to increase the number of skilled engineers or managers open to new technology, both essential to boosting competitiveness (Daly, 1991).   As noted above, transfer of technology continued to be limited to a relatively small number of sectors. Finally, the distribution system for technology and goods were both found to be substantially deficient in the ability to serve a larger economy.

In an effort to improve the export capability of the economy, the Mexican government has looked to support areas that will develop a sustainable base.   Research has shown that two of the main elements in creating an export-driven economy are innovation and technological learning, leading to several waves of product introductions and process innovations.   The failure or success of countries competing in international markets is closely related to the way in which the productive structure, the technological and political policies, and the innovating institutions interact.   This interaction has been researched from the point of view of stimulating function through supportive governmental programming, or the opposite, the activities of innovation and technological learning carried out by companies (Aboites, 1994).   The great majority of literature on Mexican science and technology reflects the support of government planning, with little focus on the role of the firm.   This is not an unexpected result in light of the focus on import substitution policy with a clear leading role for the government.   In the future, the encouragement of innovative activities by firms must be highlighted to strengthen Mexico's competitiveness.   Accordingly, the role of the government must shift from provider of technology to facilitator of technology transfer.

The Mexican government has recognized the need for a change in the role it plays and has made several key changes to move in that direction. Mexican commercial policy was also revised during the past two decades to regulate the flow of external technology to ration the cost of that technology in the current account, although many of these regulations were dropped in the 1990s (Whiting, 1991). In essence, the Mexican government was searching for a remedy to the external imbalance due to rapid growth of imports of capital and intermediate goods. A key aspect of the new commercial policy included the reduction of import taxes and tariffs on capital goods, as is evidenced by the lowering of the average import tariff from 13.3 percent in 1985 to 5.6 percent in 1987 (OECD, 1994). This measure temporarily reinforced economic protectionism, further delaying the effective opening of the Mexican market (Aboites, 1994). Many observers of the Mexican economy predicted large gains through the opening of the market to international competition following NAFTA, with many estimates predicting real growth in excess of five percent per year, but few highlighted the difficulties that were to face the Mexican industrial sector during the first few years of increased import competition. Many firms were simply unable to compete, forcing the closure of many businesses with the displacement of many Mexican workers.

The new neoliberal economic changes highlighted the need for new science and technology policies to be carried out by the government to remedy the imbalance in the economy. While the pre-aperatura, or prior to the opening of the economy, commercial policy emphasized a protectionist character, the new science and technology policy has been opened through governmental and institutional actions over the last twenty years. Nonetheless, the science and technology policy continues to be geared toward internally creating the capacity to generate technology adequate for the needs and conditions of the country. To reach the science and technology objectives, institutional legislative actions were carried out to regulate the most significant international flows of technology. The reform of the Law of Foreign Investment, Transfer of Technology, Patents, and Trademarks is an example of these legislative actions (Aboites, 1994).

The changes in policy were further reflected by different government postures in macroeconomic policy. The 1980s post recession crisis can be divided into two periods: 1982-1987, and 1988-1994. In the first period, the intention was to have a gradual commercial liberalization with different mechanisms used to facilitate payment of the foreign debt. It is generally accepted that the first strategy did not work. Results of the program included high social costs, lower real salaries, lower public expenditures and a growing government deficit, increased inequality of income, high inflation rates, general uncertainty, and relatively low levels of investment and economic growth (Dussel, 1995).

The strategy changed at the end of 1987 with the introduction of the neoliberal economic model. The industrial policy beginning in 1988 was characterized by its "horizontal" style. In other words, it affected all of the manufacturing industries, so as not to create conflicts between competing sectors. The principal mechanisms of the new industrial strategy included economic deregulation, the elimination of sectoral programs, and the rationalization of fiscal stimuli. In the second period, Mexico witnessed an accelerated liberalization and initiated industrialization directed at exports. The new liberalization strategy gave priority to inflation control, reduction of the fiscal deficit, and encouragement of foreign investment. The process also included reduction in tariffs and privatization of many government enterprises, with the notable exception of the politically sensitive petrochemical sector. The macroeconomic change was aimed at the creation of not only economic growth but structural transformation of industrial sectors. The privatized industrial firms were to become leaders in the development of an export-driven economy, similar to the model of the Southeast Asian countries. The combination of foreign investment, coupled with inexpensive labor and energy, were thought to be sufficient to finance the neoliberal economic model (Dussel, 1995).

The macroeconomic strategy required two fundamental elements, exchange rates and real interest rates, to control inflation and attract foreign investment. First, the exchange rate was placed on a path of slow and steady depreciation, although relatively high interest rates were maintained to slow inflation and retain capital inflows into the country. Inflation was rapidly reduced, falling below ten percent per year by 1993.[2] Unfortunately, inflation returned in 1995 following the devaluation of the peso. The decrease in inflation during the period from 1996 to 1998 was a sign that the Mexican government has recognized the need to control money supply and debt. In general, an expectation of steady and reasonable government action in the control of macroeconomic policy was created during the period prior to the devaluation in 1994, but most of that confidence was lost following the surprise devaluation. At the same time, the Mexican government indicated that the exchange rate would be a primary tool in the restructuring of the economy. This led to lower inflation, but did not sufficiently prepare the economy to compete with a rapid influx of imported capital and consumer goods. Inflation was under control, but the competitive infrastructure lacked incentive to upgrade worker skills or invest in new capital equipment. See Figure 3.2.

FIGURE 3.2

CHANGE IN MEXICAN CONSUMER PRICES
PERCENT, 1980 - 1997

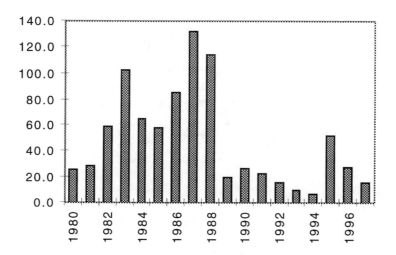

Source: INEGI

However, the rate of devaluation was insufficient to cover the difference between the relative domestic and foreign prices, causing an overvaluation of the real exchange rate. The strong peso caused considerable difficulty in the implementation of the liberalization plan. There was drastic growth of manufactured and consumer good imports, coupled with a reduction in the exportation of manufactured goods. Clearly the Mexican economy was not importing the appropriate capital goods and technology needed to create a modern export sector. Rather, the economy was becoming increasingly oriented toward the consumer-oriented demand pattern found in the United States. Mexican exports, not including the maquiladoras, grew at an average annual rate of 5.8 percent from 1988 - 1992; however, this was considerably lower when compared to the 1982 - 1987 export growth rate of 24.2 percent. Although the surprise 1994 peso devaluation again increased the rate of exportation, the Mexican government must find a method other than manipulation of exchange rates if it hopes to sustain export growth in a variety of sectors in support of economic development. As Porter

(1990) notes, "Cheap labor and a favorable exchange rate are not meaningful definitions of competitiveness." The manipulation of exchange rates in search of long-run competitiveness is destined to meet with failure (Shapiro, 1996). See Figure 3.3.

FIGURE 3.3

CHANGE IN MEXICAN EXPORTS AND IMPORTS,
PERCENT, 1980 - 1997

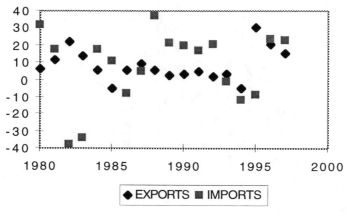

Source: INEGI

The slowdown in exports likely reflects the drastic effect of macroeconomic liberalization on the internal added value of labor. Although Mexican labor was and continues to be relatively inexpensive compared to labor in the United States, continued unemployment and underemployment problems have led to lower productivity that largely offsets the labor cost advantage (Dussel, 1995). At the same time other nations, such as China, are increasingly able to export low technology goods using labor with much lower wage rates than those found in Mexico. Mexico is unable to compete effectively in the market for these goods, nor can Mexico compete with the upscale goods that require high technology for manufacture. As such, Mexico is stuck in the middle between the very low cost producers of goods in the Third World and the high technology manufacturers of the First World. Unable to return to competitiveness solely through low wages and an undervalued peso, Mexico must continue to develop the capability to compete with the more advanced industrial nations.

Second, foreign investment was vital to continue paying the foreign debt, which had steadily risen during the past decade. The attraction of direct foreign investment could only be accomplished by offering stable macroeconomic expectations, a high real interest rate, and the certainty that there would not be a devaluation. In addition, the relatively high real interest rates used by the United States to guard against inflation continue to raise the cost of financing Mexico's debt, much of which is denominated in dollars. As the deficit in the current account steadily increased, the total foreign debt went from 99 million dollars in 1988 to 142 billion dollars in 1993. The increasing debt service load grew to unsustainable levels in the face of rising interest rates in both Mexico and the United States. When Mexican banks needed to attract even more foreign investment, they imposed even higher real interest rates (Dussel, 1995). Unfortunately, the Mexican financial system was not ready to absorb severe shocks to the system, and the devaluation of December 1994 became a painful reality. See Figure 3.4.

FIGURE 3.4

MEXICAN FOREIGN DEBT
BILLIONS OF DOLLARS, 1980 - 1997

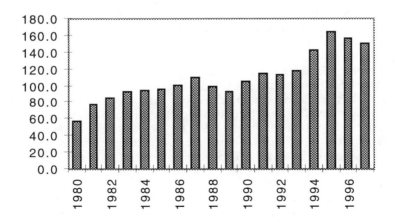

Source: INEGI

The result of the industrial policy during the liberalization process revealed three crucial aspects. First, liberalization by itself is not sufficient to develop and maintain a strategy for development. Other steps were required to create linkages between government, business, and the external environment, as the neoliberal policies had not created mechanisms for creation of linkages. Second, the liberalization lacked coherence and consistency between the macroeconomic and the sectoral strategies. Several industries were left out of modernization efforts as the focus continually returned to the parastatal firms, particularly Pemex. The Mexican economy simply could not sustain growth while undergoing a wide range of drastic structural changes. Third, the liberalization suggested a deep incompatibility with industrialization oriented to exports with respect to the existing economic base. The Mexican economy continued to look to satisfy internal markets before foreign markets, and to import high levels of consumer goods rather than capital, technology, and intermediate goods (Dussel, 1995).

As a result, the Mexican government took several actions aimed at supporting the development of an advanced technological infrastructure, led by the National Development Plan of 1989-1994. One of the goals of the National Development Plan was to achieve the integration of Mexico into the world economy through the modernization of the productive plant and the strengthening of the exporting sector. The program diagnosed internal structural problems that generated high costs and low levels of quality, but Mexican technology continued to fall behind. There was an inefficient assignment of resources, which in turn limited the capacity of growth and development of the economy. The programs and strategies of the National Development Plan include as the four principal objectives the defense of sovereignty and promotion of Mexican interests in the world, increased democratic participation, support of the economic recovery with price stability, and an increase in the economic welfare of the people (Aguilar, 1995). These lofty goals are politically palatable, but clearly do not follow the Asian model of economic development prior to an opening of the political process.

Under the National Development Plan, another sub-program was developed to function from 1991 to 1994, the Program for the Modernization and Development of the Micro, Small and Medium-sized Enterprises, or PROMIP. This program acknowledges the importance of these three types of companies because they represent 98 percent of the companies dealing with industrial transformation, they absorb more than 50 percent of the labor force, and they provide 43 percent of the manufactured products and 11 percent of the GNP. The micro, small, and medium companies are found in all the areas of Mexican manufacturing; however, more than 60 percent of these companies deal with food, metal products, printing and publishing, and non-metallic mineral production. There is also a notable economic and demographic concentration because 61 percent of these companies can be found in the

Mexican population centers of Mexico City, Jalisco, Nuevo Leon, Guanajuato, Puebla and Veracruz (Sanchez, 1993). The PROMIP had six objectives: to strengthen the growth of micro, small, and medium-sized businesses via qualitative changes in the way purchasing, production and commercialization were done, with the idea to reinforce its presence in domestic and international markets; to increase the technological level and quality; to deepen the measures of deregulation, decentralization, and administrative simplification; to promote the establishment of such enterprises in the whole country to contribute to the regional development, to support deconcentration and preserve the environment; to promote the creation of productive and permanent jobs; and to encourage investment in the social sector to promote manufacturing activities (Aguilar, 1995).

Other governmental agencies were also responsible for leading roles in the new technology strategy. For example, the Secretaria de Hacienda y Credito Publico, the Mexican Treasury Department, and Nacional Financiera helped to create credit mechanisms to facilitate the access to specialized technological services. The service given to micro and small enterprises has grown dramatically during the past decade. Approximately 11 thousand firms received aid in 1989, of which 55 percent were micro and 38 percent were small. The program grew to serve 93 thousand firms in 1993, of which 62 percent were micro and 36 percent were small. In the case of the small business, they receive aid to contract accounting firms and accounting, legal and administrative consulting (Aguilar, 1995).

The strategy of the government programs is to create policies that promote entrepreneurial organizations based on the coordination of the different government offices and an agreement to work in concert with the industrialists. The objectives of the program include strengthening the growth of smaller companies, making qualitative changes in the purchasing, production, and sales methods, increasing the technological level and productivity, fostering regional development and decentralization, and promoting a better income distribution and the investment in manufacturing activities. The use of market analysis of projects and the requirement of matching private funds signal that the government and industry have now concluded that government direction of technology policy is not likely to succeed (Micheli, 1996). Unfortunately, many businesses in Mexico continue to assume that CONACYT will drive technological policy and implementation. To reach these objectives, entrepreneurial initiative and talent will need to be supported through changes in organizational structure, increased participation in the exporting process, and the development of new forms of financing (Sanchez, 1993).

The problems of Mexican industry are related to a series of flaws that range from insufficient national and international investment to a lack of coordination between the public and private sector, the lack of opportune and fast information on the economic opportunities derived from trade, and international protectionism.   Excessive regulations, federal and state transport and freight, customs functioning, establishment of new firms and access to intermediate goods, and normalization have resulted in high and unnecessary costs, which have negatively influenced productivity and the allotment of resources. Recent government studies and programs have pointed out the problems related to the maquiladora industry and the border zone, the high concentration of regional productivity and the problems of the micro, small, and medium enterprises, unlike the National Program for Development. In particular, the smaller enterprises face constraints that include limited capacity to negotiate and to organize, an inadequate technological level, and insufficient qualification of labor force, which result in low levels of productivity; the markets are regional in nature, and have serious difficulties entering export markets, as their volume and production quality can not compete in the international arena; and there is also insufficient institutional financing, lack of physical infrastructure and indispensable services, and excessive regulation or controls (Aguilar, 1995).

---

[1] Data obtained from the Human Development Report 1997, Table 1 and Table 17.

[2] It is notable that the print and electronic media paid a great deal of attention to this governmental goal during 1993, dutifully reporting the progress toward a single digit inflation rate. It is quite possible that this intense media attention contributed to support for the government's program; however, it may have also encouraged the government to keep the value of the peso artificially high throughout 1994 even though it became increasingly apparent that the peso was significantly overvalued.   It remains to be seen whether Mexico will again return to a policy of substantially overvaluing the peso, leading to another round of devaluations.

Chapter 4

Technology Transfer Strategy and Law

The role of the Mexican government in encouraging technological development has changed dramatically since 1983. Its intervention, in 1970-1982, caused the creation of a governmental protectionist system featuring foreign investment control and the registration of transfer of technology. The government also directly promoted a policy of domestic technology development. In the period 1983-1991, the state regulations moved away from import substitution and looked to encourage more participation of private enterprises, and to promote formation of risk capital (Aboites, 1994). Mexico's strategy now includes importation of technology from abroad instead of trying to develop it entirely in Mexico. The development of technology has also been increasingly directed toward academia and away from industry (Moss, 1990). The next critical step will be the creation of policy driven by industrial needs in which academia plays a key role by supplying the necessary basic research and highly trained researchers and engineers.

In the earlier period of technology regulation by the government, beginning in 1973, technology transfer law in Mexico emphasized that all agreements for the transfer of technology into Mexico first be submitted to the National Registry of the Transfer of Technology and subsequently be approved by the Ministry of Commerce and Industrial Development. Limited exemptions were provided for advisory and consulting services provided abroad for a total duration of less than six months. Registration was the first step in a lengthy and sometimes confusing governmental merit review process. Many exemptions to technology transfer law in Mexico were allowable at the discretion of the governmental reviewing agency. These exemptions included technology transfer programs that created permanent jobs, improved technical qualifications of human resources, manufactured new products in Mexico, improved Mexico's balance of payments, decreased unit production costs, developed domestic suppliers, or initiated new research and development programs (O'Brien, 1991). The wide discretion of the government bureaucracy only added to frustration for those applying for permits, which was reinforced by the cultural acceptance of the payment of bribes.

Since 1983, Mexico has followed several objectives in the administration of technology transfer, including: narrowing the classes for which registration is required, remove domestic and international obstacles to technology licensing, shifting from content of each agreement to how the technology will enhance the competitiveness of Mexico, limiting government discretion in regulation of contracts, and promotion of technological modernization to develop both small and large firms using domestic technology (Moss, 1990). In summary, the responsibility for technology creation, dissemination, and assimilation was now in the domain of the private sector. Mexico's strategy focused on external technology, which became as important or more important than internal technology (Aboites, 1994).

Rather than rely totally on domestic technology, the Mexican government decided to create domestic science and technology capacities to efficiently tie into the flow of technological development in industrialized countries or from Southeast Asia. Purchase and diffusion of external technology and external investment were to become the two fundamental ways to increase international competitiveness of Mexican products. Deregulation of technology transfer and foreign investment, coupled with more security for industrial ownership, became key elements of institutionalization strategies for science and technology (Aboites, 1994). Mexico even was willing to discontinue screening of foreign direct investment under the terms of NAFTA, but was unable to convince Canada to adopt the same posture (Graham and Krugman, 1995). Unfortunately, the efforts to reform the legal and political structure for technology did not rapidly lead to widespread structural changes in manufacturing output, although certain sectors have benefited through acquisition of new technology (UNCTC, 1992).

Three types of modifications took place during the 1983-1991 period, reflecting the dissatisfaction with the results of the 1970-1982 period. First, government regulations and procedures were revised. The import permit was eliminated, along with the National Registry for Technology Transfer and the National Registry of Foreign Investment. This essentially reduced the bureaucratic obstacles to importation of foreign technology. Second, the private sector was charged with programs that formerly were administered by government offices. Greater involvement by the business community was viewed as likely to encourage business to business linkages with foreign entities. Third, and most importantly, Mexico enthusiastically joined the cooperative structure of the world economy, as demonstrated by membership in the General Agreement on Trade and Tariffs, or GATT, and later by the signing of the North American Free Trade Agreement, or NAFTA. Under the GATT and NAFTA, policy was revised to encourage formation of risk capital to be used for research and development activities. As a charter member of the World Trade Organization, the successor to the GATT, Mexico continues to commit to working toward liberal economic policy. This step clearly aided in removing many of the significant difficulties and obstacles that Mexican firms had experienced in raising capital for modernization efforts, including the importation of technology (Aboites, 1994).

Two legislative changes affecting industrial ownership took place from 1983-1991. The first was the passage of changes to the Law of Inventions and Trademarks. The second was a deep legislative reform through the Promotion and Protection of Industrial Ownership Law in light of NAFTA negotiations, altering regulations about patent exploitation and import licenses. In the original 1976 legislation, these regulations were an obstacle for foreign enterprises that make use of the national industrial ownership system to protect themselves from domestic competition. After 1991, foreign patent makers had more protection. The test of technical novelty to certify the nature of the innovation can now be done in foreign offices, while previously it had to be done locally. The 1991 legislation included the elimination of patent restrictions on food, pharmaceutical, biotechnology, medicine, and other products. Also, the right of the Mexican government to expropriate patents was eliminated. The penalties were not modified, but tighter controls were established against industrial piracy (Aboites, 1994). Unfortunately, many of the new regulations have not been effectively enforced, leading to ongoing political battles between the U.S. and Mexican governments, particularly with respect to piracy of intellectual property (Preston, 1996).

In the past, foreign investors frequently complained about the lack of security in the system of industrial ownership in Mexico. The patents in industrialized countries last around twenty years, while in

Mexico they lasted only ten years. As a result, the number of Mexican patents issued was very small when contrasted with the technological level already present in the country (Corona, 1994). Further, Mexican nationals are not fully participating in the move toward increased patenting. Although the total number of patent applications in Mexico has more than doubled since 1984, the number of applications by Mexican nationals has remained flat (Castañeda and Toledo Barraza, 1994). Foreign investors also complained about the inadequate protection of intellectual property and the lack of severe punishment for industrial piracy. Due to this, research and development activities, as well as transfer of technology carried out by domestic and foreign companies in Mexico, were relatively low. The problem was not only the inefficiency of institutions and instruments for science and technology, but also the different role assigned to the science and technology community within the newly industrialized model and institutional context. This new technological concept was closely related to the competitive role enterprises would have to play in the international market, and the nature of the new technological paradigm widely promoted in the 1980s. The government proposal for the new science and technology strategy can be summarized as encouraging the private sector to become an active participant in the technological process, deregulation and protection of industrial ownership to increase the flow of external technology, and creation of easier ways for the productive sector to assimilate foreign and domestic technology (Aboites, 1994).

As seen in TABLE 4.3, Mexico's granting of patents lags behind the economic cycle, with relatively few patents issued as compared to those issued in the developed nations and leading newly industrializing economies, such as Taiwan and South Korea. A direct comparison with patenting activity in South Korea illustrates the clear difference in the tendency to patent. In 1970, South Koreans applied for 1,202 patents and Mexicans applied for 750. By 1985, the gap had widened to 2,702 applications by South Korean inventors compared to 612 by Mexican nationals. By 1991, the gap had opened to 13,255 South Korean applications versus only 564 Mexican applications. Mexican patenting activity actually dropped by 1995, resulting in only 436 applications (World Bank, 1998). The same pattern is observed in the awarding of US patents to foreign applicants. In 1992, the South Koreans were awarded 586 U.S. patents, while Mexican nationals were awarded only 45 (Castañeda and Toledo Barraza, 1994).

The relatively low usage of patents has created an environment where patenting is not valued by industry, with less than ten percent of technology used by industry tied to Mexican patents (Pfaff et al, 1993).

Mexican firms lack the necessary background to know how to write patents that cannot be circumvented by third parties, leading to a cultural reluctance to file for patents. Further, research centers and universities did not have confidence in the government's support for patent holders in defense against infringement, leading to a reluctance to patent new technology (Camacho, 1994). Further, the relatively high number of small and micro enterprises also works against patenting by Mexicans. It can be argued that the complexity of modern technology favors the larger formal organizations over individual inventors and innovators. For the larger firms, in-house research dominates, providing the in-house absorptive capacity to "recognize, evaluate, negotiate, and finally adapt the technology" available from other businesses and the academic sector (Dosi, 1988).

TABLE 4.1

MEXICO PATENT APPLICATIONS AND PATENTS GRANTED,
1980 - 1990

Year	Applications	Granted
1980	4,797	1,996
1981	5,328	2,210
1982	4,806	2,583
1983	4,095	2,247
1984	4,003	1,737
1985	3,700	1,172
1986	3,865	987
1987	4,251	1,156
1988	4,400	3,158
1989	4,574	2,141
1990	5,061	1,620
Total	48,880	21,007

Source: SECOFI, Indicadores: Actividades científicas y tecnológicas, 1991.

Fortunately, recent reforms are improving the intellectual property environment. The passage of the Law for the Protection of Industrial Property, or LFPPI, in 1991 and the repeal of the National Registry for the Transfer of Technology have initiated a new enthusiasm for patenting in Mexico. In 1992, 6961 patent applications were filed, with 565 applications originating with Mexican nationals. This represents a 30 percent increase over the 5271 applications for 1991. By 1993, 8212 applications were filed (Camacho, 1994). Nonetheless, foreigners control over ninety percent of all patents issued in Mexico. In contrast, foreigners control nearly half of all patents issued in the United States (National Science Board, 1993).

An additional problem with patenting in Mexico has been the slow pace of patent examination. Prior to 1991, only 55 percent of all patent applications were examined within three years. Thirty-three percent were examined between four and six years, and 12 percent had to wait between 7 and 12 years. By 1993, following the new government mandates, 80 percent of all patent applications were examined by the end of the third year (Camacho, 1994). Approximately four percent of all patent applications continue to wait between seven and eleven years for review (Castañeda and Toledo Barraza, 1994).

Chapter 5

Government Support for Science and Technology

Mexico's government dominates science and technology creation and dissemination programs much more completely than do other emerging economy governments. During the past decade, the Mexican government has provided approximately seventy-eight percent of all financial support for domestic science and technology programs. Industry follows with approximately twenty-one percent, and higher education trails with slightly more than one percent. Of the federal spending, sixty-three percent is administered by the Secretariat of Public Education, or SEP, which in 1993 provided forty-five percent of its funds to the National Council for Science and Technology, commonly known as CONACYT. The national university, UNAM, received approximately twenty-one percent. CONACYT and the UNAM share about forty percent of all federal science and technology funding, effectively concentrating most of the funds into the Mexico City area (OECD, 1994).

Industry continues to receive a minor share of the limited government spending for science and technology. From 1988 to 1991, the money spent on science and technology had the following break down: scientific and technological areas in the academic world, 30.4 percent; development of farming and forestry, 16.2 percent; regulation of the National System for Science and Technology, 15.2 percent; production and distribution of energy, 13.9 percent; and industrial development, 11.5 percent (Aboites, 1994). The period 1987 - 1991 witnessed a drastic fall of expenditures on industrial development and farming. Activities related to administrative costs grew considerably, while activities closely related to production and technology development decreased. The government bureaucracy continued to absorb a substantial share of available funds, largely at the expense of support for industrial technology programs.

The area where expenses directly related to science and technology grew was in the production and distribution of energy. Note that this trend was clearly opposed to the government's expressed desire to move away from oil exportation as a mainstay of the economy. With the high level of targeted funding, the "Instituto Mexicano del Petroleo" and "Instituto de Investigaciones Electricas" play an important role in research and development. The former has a high level of patent production and the latter has been successful in technological development. As a result, a few select institutions control most of the research capacity. For example, in the area of engineering the national petroleum and electrical institutes hire 60 percent of all masters and doctoral students in their respective academic areas. This increases the concentration in the areas of research, with more than 50 percent of the projects focusing on agriculture, medicine, and biology (Molina, 1995). Further, a review of the results originating from this strategy shows that financing has not been directed to productive activities (except production and distribution of energy); it has largely been directed to administrative and academic activities (Aboites, 1994).

The Secretariat of Public Education, or SEP, has the highest level of responsibility for coordination and administration of science and technology programs in Mexico. Most of SEP's science and technology operations are carried out through CONACYT. Mexico's policy structure differs greatly in this respect from the other major industrial nations, which do not have a central government office responsible for technology policy, preferring to spread the responsibility between several agencies (Ostry and Nelson, 1995).

Founded in 1971, CONACYT is the leader in the government's effort to develop a cohesive science and technology policy. CONACYT receives 27 percent of all federal outlays for science and technology, with the remaining funds committed to other secretariats. Roughly one half of the federal funds are used to support R&D activities, followed by science and technology education and technical services (OECD, 1994). Initially, its functions were to support national research and technological development and to promote increase the number of personnel capable of working to create and sustain the national scientific and technology abilities. A major step in this process was the publication of the First National Plan for Science and Technology in 1976. Several science and technology instruments were created, and the Law of Patents and Marks was subsequently reformed. However, there was a paradox during the 1970-1981 period: the budget assigned to Science and Technology reached its maximum level, but during the same period the flow of external technology showed an unprecedented growth. From 1970-1976 the average mean growth to purchase machinery and equipment was 5.2 percent, while it increased to 33.1 percent from 1977 to 1981. CONACYT assigned a great portion of its budget to the formation of human resources, especially outside Mexico. From 1977 to 1982, the original objectives to ration the external flow of technology and to create infrastructure and the endogenous technical capacity were ignored (Patel, 1993).

The deep economic crisis of 1982 and the lengthy recession that followed caused radical changes in the economic policy, including policy toward science and technology. The following funds were restructured or created in the period from 1988 to 1992: Reinforcement of Scientific and Technological Infrastructure; Retention and Repatriation of Mexican Researchers; The Creation of Lectures of Excellence; and Projects of Scientific Research. The series of changes culminated with the further restructuring of CONACYT in 1989 with creation of the Counseling Committee. In the last ten years, the policy for science and technology has witnessed significant change, following the guidance of CONACYT's strategic goals.

CONACYT has four central goals for the development of science and technology programs: to establish decentralized decision-making capability for the scientific, government, and private sectors; encourage rapid growth in the number of research and development personnel, creation of a scientific culture in Mexico, and to support of technological development to support the country's overall development plan, providing the benefits of science and technology to all sectors of the economy. As such, CONACYT's strategy for Mexico centers around giving technology a "deliberate push" through injection of massive doses of education and training, especially in engineering and training of the labor force at the small business level. CONACYT recognizes that this has produced some unwanted side effects, such as "brain drain" and opposition to traditional sources of political and economic power. The major components of the CONACYT science and technology program include scholarships, industry programs, centers for research, and international agreements, such as those with the National Science Foundation in the United States and the Centre

National de la Recherche Scientifique in France.   Additional cost sharing of the programs by the private sector is required if sufficient resources are to be supplied to a broad range of programs.

CONACYT's programs with higher education give preference to master's level work at Mexican institutions, while most doctoral and post-doctoral studies are done abroad.   During the past twenty years, efforts have been made to decentralize academic work away from Mexico City.   These efforts, while making limited progress, have not significantly diminished the dominance of Mexico City in the national academic arena.   This will take considerable political will, noting the heavy influence of the national university, the Autonomous National University of Mexico, or UNAM, on higher education programs throughout the country.   The UNAM enrolls a high proportion of all graduate students in Mexico, and has been involved in the accreditation of degree programs in universities throughout Mexico.   An example of the resulting education bottleneck is that only the UNAM grants doctorates in business administration in Mexico.   Other leading institutions, such as the Instituto Tecnologico de Estudios Superior de Monterrey, or ITESM, have begun joint doctoral programs with U.S. institutions to avoid this restriction.   The higher education programs of CONACYT and the Mexican government have met with considerable criticism, such as that of Patel, "It is not understood that the mere expansion of human and financial resources for scientific and technological activities does not ensure necessarily science and technology advancement.   The progress in this respect depends more on linking educational, productive, and scientific / technological systems than on the politically acceptable distribution of money to the existing isolated institutional structures or distributing scholarships abroad at random."

An important aspect of the reform effort is to determine up to what point these changes affect the National System of Innovation, or NSI. A National System of Innovation has been defined as a "set of distinct institutions which jointly and individually contribute to the development and diffusion of new technologies and which provides the frameworks within which governments form and implement policies to influence the innovation process."   The NSI in Mexico has been, and continues to be, driven by government policy and the UNAM. Technological systems, on the other hand, are defined as "networks of agents interacting in each specific technology area under a particular institutional infrastructure for the purpose of generating, diffusing, and utilizing technology."   Technological systems differ from national systems of innovation in that they are defined by technology rather than national boundaries, they vary from one technology area to another within a country, and in the microeconomic emphasis given to diffusion and utilization of technology (Carlsson, 1994). The NSI system in Mexico includes the enterprises and the networks that establish ties between enterprises and other institutions, and the institutional structure that generates different patterns of inputs and restrictions for the productive system (Aboites, 1994).

A significant positive step in the drive to encourage more careers in academic and industrial research was the creation of the National System of Investigators, or SNI (Rudomín, 1994). Although the SNI is only slightly over a decade old, it plays a key role in supporting and challenging researchers to increase the quality of scientific research. Membership in the SNI grew from 1,396 in 1984 to 6,233 in 1993, while engineering and technical membership in the SNI has approximately tripled since 1984 to about two thousand members (Peña Díaz, 1994). The birth of the SNI was not seen as a new concept in Mexico, but was viewed as an extension of practices in many OECD countries. The SNI was to serve as a national technological system with contributions from and benefits to industry, government, and academia (Greene, 1994).

The changes to improve support for Mexican technological development must originate from within Mexico, with a modest supportive role for foreign companies. A limited amount of support for Mexican science and technology programs originates in the United States, with activity centered around the National Science Foundation, or NSF, among other agencies. Total spending by NSF related to Latin America was approximately $42 million in 1990, but because of the "international component" to the spending, there is no breakdown of how much of the spending is actually supports research in Latin America. The Agency for International Development's Caribbean and Latin American Scholarship Program, or CLASP, provided training for 27 thousand people between 1985 and 1996. In addition, even hundred Fulbright scholars from Latin America study and research in the United States each year (U.S. House, 1992). Unfortunately, U.S. federal budget constraints will likely reduce the number of scholars participating in these programs.

Chapter 6

Technology Transfer by Universities and Incubator Programs

With the beginning of the neoliberal transformation of the Mexican economy in 1983, a new industrialization pattern became associated with substantial modifications in the educational strategy for science and technology. This change of strategy was necessitated by the lack of efficient institutions and instruments for science and technology. Mexico's import substitution policy had simply not created a basis to meet the technological requirements of the new model of global industrial competition. Mexico's General Agreement on Trade and Tariffs, or GATT, membership in 1986 and the signing of the North American Free Trade Agreement augmented the shifts in science and technology policy required for the shift to the neoliberal economic model. Mexico's current membership in the World Trade Organization will continue to apply substantial pressure for transformation of science and technology policy.

Education appears to provide the greatest contribution to country growth rates when compared to other labor force factors, such as gender and unemployment. The social factors, such as education and investment, provide a capability to absorb new technology in an effort to "catch up" to other nations. For example, growth in the United States high technology industries has been attributed to prolonged investment in public and private education, coupled with modern R&D departments in corporations and large public investments in high technology industry following World War II (Fagerberg, 1994). Mexico assumed that the growth of the economy would automatically encourage development of educational policy supportive of increased technological capacity, both in higher education and in the provision of skills for use by industry. The government shifted spending to support increased educational opportunities, increasing public expenditures for education from 4.7 percent of GDP during the 1980s to 5.3 percent of GDP during the 1990s (World Bank, 1998).

When growth did not provide development of the educational and training system, Mexico was faced with shortages of technicians and skilled professionals with sufficient training to modernize the industrial sector (Patel, 1993).   The OECD estimates that Mexico has 9.4 scientists and engineers for every ten thousand workers.   Of these workers, fifty percent work in the government sector and forty-nine percent in higher education. Only one percent of all engineers work in industry or non-profit institutions.   The UNAM alone employs ten percent of all scientists and engineers in Mexico.   Private higher education employs relatively few researchers (OECD, 1994).   The industrial sector not only faces a shortage of technical personnel, it faces a nearly complete absence of qualified technical personnel. Consequently, it will take an extended number of years to create a core of technical personnel in the private sector.

The low number of faculty and students trained under the import substitution program has led to ongoing difficulty in creating a qualified labor market, both in academia and in industry. Only three percent of all state public institution faculty hold the doctoral degree, with approximately fifteen percent holding a masters degree.   In many institutions, the majority of faculty are holders of baccalaureate degrees (Barros Valero, 1994). The situation is slightly better for the leading private institutions, which have continued to augment their faculty with foreign scholars. Further, most of the faculty holding the doctorate are research faculty with limited teaching duties.   With such a limited availability of highly qualified faculty, meeting the challenge of providing qualified engineers and technicians for the developing industrial base has proven to be an elusive goal for Mexican higher education institutions.

Even as compared to other industrializing nations, Mexico compares poorly in the provision of higher education opportunities. For example, the percentage of Mexicans in higher education is less than one-half the comparable level for South Korea (Grunwald, 1991). The disparity is even greater for engineering students, with South

Korea's universities graduating five times as many engineers per capita as do Mexico's universities (Lall, 1992).   At the graduate level, the disparity becomes even greater. Mexico has approximately two masters level graduates and 0.10 doctoral program graduates for every one hundred thousand population. This compares to nineteen masters level graduates and five doctoral graduates per one hundred thousand population in the United States. Of every one hundred students entering Mexican universities, only ten complete their initial program of study, and three enter graduate studies. At the doctoral level, only fourteen out of every one hundred students enrolled ever complete the program. In addition, only 4.1 percent of all doctoral students are enrolled in engineering and technology programs (Molina, 1995).   Although the university system enrolls thousands of students annually, it is clear that recent efforts to move more students toward successful completion of an undergraduate degree are still lacking.

Further complicating the problem, Mexican researchers are highly clustered around Mexico City, with sixty percent of all research and development personnel and more than fifty percent of all projects located in the capital city. In 1992, fourteen percent of all baccalaureate degrees and a stunning ninety-five percent of all doctorates awarded in Mexico originated at the UNAM (OECD, 1994).   The inexpensive tuition, supported through a generous reading of the Mexican Constitution, continues to encourage high matriculation rates without forcing the issue of quality education in Mexico City or the states (Lorey, 1996). The drive to increase regional opportunities in education is underway, and the states received increased responsibility for education from the 1993 Agreement for the Modernization of Education. Included with the responsibility was increased local control over spending options (OECD, 1996).   Nonetheless, the lion's share of funding and government attention is directed toward leading institutions in Mexico City.

The use of foreign study has also been unable to create a sufficiently large educated labor force, even when compared to other recently industrializing nations.   Ten times more Koreans and forty times more Taiwanese than Mexicans received engineering and science Ph.D. degrees in the United States between 1960 and 1988 (Grunwald, 1991). Without more technology capability in the management ranks, Mexico's progress in creating an environment supporting industrial innovation appears to be restricted.   Part of the loss of U.S. technological leadership has been attributed to the diminishing number of senior managers with technical backgrounds, as compared to managers in Germany and Japan (Porter, 1990). Clearly, Mexico is in an even more difficult in finding technical managers as a result of having a much smaller base of technically trained personnel.

Some of the problems in the development of an educated base of engineers derives from the historical roots of the Mexican education system.   The dominant model for Latin American education derives from the French Napoleonic system, which focuses on teaching and professional education. This is in contrast with the research university focus in the United States, Great Britain, and the developing economies of the Far East (Alcántara Santuario, 1994).   The different focus of education is reflected in the tendency of authors to publish in journals. Mexican authors have published slightly more than one thousand articles per year in international publications since 1980, ranking third in Latin America behind Brazil and Argentina.   U.S. authors, by comparison, publish several hundred thousand professional articles per year (Aréchiga, 1994).   This difficulty is partially countered by the increasing tendency of Mexican authors to publish jointly with foreign co-authors.   Approximately thirty-four percent of Mexican journal articles published in 1990 had a foreign co-author, up from 18.5 percent in 1980. The majority of co-authors were from the United States, and the Mexican authors were typically from the northwest or southern regions of the country (Russell, 1995). Clearly, researchers away from Mexico City have been more inclined to cooperate with foreign co-authors. This indicates that joint research will likely increase as the educational system is decentralized. The topics of the research are also likely to reflect the regional needs to a greater degree, increasing the applicability of the research programs to local industry.

Another critical concern is the lack of ties between industry and the government centers for research and development. It has been argued that Mexican industry cannot become competitive without significant development of industrial - academic linkages (see, for example, Gutiérrez Camposeco, 1994; Martuscelli and Soberón, 1994). Mexico, like any industrial nation, needs to connect specialized research institutes to industrial clusters as a means of increasing the amount and effectiveness of R&D activity (Porter, 1990). In the past, less than four percent of university research projects were related to private industry.   For example, private enterprises did not make use of technological information available from the Mexican government, preferring to avoid bureaucratic delays. Information searches were rarely employed, with less than 250 searches conducted annually. In addition, available funding was underutilized because Mexican entrepreneurs used only eighteen percent of the available Fiscal Promotion Certificates (Aboites, 1994).   Many entrepreneurs simply lack the time and knowledge base to effectively navigate the complex bureaucratic structure that the government has arranged for administration of aid programs to smaller businesses.

A significant positive step toward the development of industry - academic linkages in Mexico is the founding of technology incubator programs similar to those in the United States. The technology development programs seek to create a linkage of the Mexican industries into the global economy by aligning production activities with professional education and research (Marín, 1993). In October 1992 the Mexican Association for Business Incubators and Technological Parks, or AMIEPAT, was formed, reflecting the growing interest in creating technology centers around the country (Villalvazo, 1994). Sponsorship of the incubator programs is coordinated between CONACYT in Mexico and the National Science Foundation in the United States. The main purpose of these programs is to provide sources of technology and financing for implementation, with small and medium companies targeted as a complement to the efforts of the larger multinational corporations (Ruiz and Garza, 1993).Mexico had ten business incubators functioning in 1994, and hoped to double that number by 1995. The great majority, 84 percent of the industrial incubators in Mexico, aim to assist agriculture, automobile, and instrumentation firms. Additional areas of support, such as material for science related firms, are expected to develop as the notion of industrial incubators and scientific parks spreads to additional geographic areas (Corona, 1994). Many of these efforts are located in the larger cities, and as such they will have difficulty reaching industry located in remote areas of the country.

Approximately two-thirds of all Mexican industrial research and development activities are carried out inside the business. Eleven percent of studies are conducted by another business, followed by consultants, eight percent, and foreign companies, four percent. Only one percent of all research and development is conducted by public universities and three percent by private universities, indicating that industry - academia linkages for the conduct of R&D activities are rare in Mexico. Some local areas have supported "grassroots" funding of technology centers, but these types of organizations are now slowly being replaced with university - industry linkages, as is the trend globally (Cooke and Morgan, 1994). For example, apparel manufacturers have created cooperative training programs for managers. In general, linkages between research and development, academia, and production rarely exist in Mexico (Patel, 1993). See TABLE 6.1.

Universities are creating their own programs to support a wide variety of training areas for business. These include quality control, international trade, strategy, design and manufacturing, materials selection, information technology, optics, communications, and biotechnology (Villalvazo, 1994). One of the largest incubator programs is located at the Autonomous National University of Mexico, or UNAM. The Coordinating Office for Scientific Research at the UNAM lists several projects for transfer of technology including weldable steel bars; zinc, aluminum, and copper alloy "zinalco"; monitoring of mutagens in water; water pollution treatment system; agricultural technology; optoelectronic devices; and electronic data banks. Clearly, many of Mexico's research facilities are providing quality scientific studies. The difficulty remains in transferring the technology developed to the industrial sector. The incubator programs, although currently limited, hold promise as a means to build necessary linkages between academia and industry.

TABLE 6.1

LOCATION OF R&D STUDIES

Location of R&D	Percent
Same Establishment	67
Other Establishment	11
Public University	1
Private University	3
Consultant	8
Foreign Company	6
Don't Know	4

Source: STPS and INEGI, 1995

The Program for Linkages between the Academy and the Industry, PREAIN, was created for promoting participation of the organizations in the education of their human resources and benefiting both partners, the organization and the university linked. The core of this program is based on three non-mutually exclusive goals of human resource education, cooperative projects of applied research, and execution of consultant work. It is important to point out that coordination between the education and the industry sectors is not easily obtained in the developing nor in the developed countries. In order to avoid the voluntary turnover of personnel from the academy to industry because of the promise of higher salaries, programs must be able to compensate earnings with extra money when the professors or researchers develop specific technological projects. Industry is required to give support to the universities in the acquisition of equipment, laboratories, computers, software and hardware. Reciprocally, the universities will provide training to the personnel working in industry. Another linkage facilitated by PREAIN is the provision of grants to students to develop their own terminal projects for obtaining either an undergraduate or a graduate degree. The program welcomes public and private higher education institutions nationwide with registration and approval by CONACYT (Marín, 1993).

Chapter 7

The Role of Micro, Small, and Medium Business

The integration of micro and small enterprises into the globalization process is one of the principal challenges to any program aimed at developing technological capability.[1] For example, modern innovation is increasingly a result of networking. Firms are increasingly relying on strategic alliances, R&D consortia, supplier - producer interfaces, and external relationships between small and large firms. This reflects the fact that large enterprises often react slowly to global changes, then need to invest considerable resources once change is required to remain competitive. On the other hand, the smaller enterprises have a powerful competitive advantage, their ability to adapt to these changes (Layne, 1993). By networking, large and small firms can compete on terms best suited to each company.

The innovation advantage of large firms lies in material advantages, resulting from a relative abundance of financial and technological resources. Small firms, on the other hand, possess behavioral advantages such as entrepreneurship, flexibility, and rapid responsiveness to a changing market environment (Rothwell, 1994). Many of the larger Mexican firms have been able to modernize their operations as a result of foreign capital infusions or joint ventures. Unfortunately, the great majority of smaller industrial firms have remained technologically dormant. This has resulted in a widespread lack of potential and realized forward and backward linkages in the manufacturing sector (Patel, 1993). Transfer of technology through linkages to suppliers are missing, providing support only for basic advances in technology even if new technology becomes available (Lall, 1992). Even if one sector modernizes, the lack of effective links into other sectors prevents the spread of modern technology into other areas of the economy.

Micro, small, and medium enterprises have played an important role in the industrialization of most countries. They are important in the advancement because they produce consumer goods for the domestic market, and supply intermediate goods and raw materials for larger companies. This is also the case in Mexico, where they represent ninety-eight percent of all firms. They have forty-nine percent of the factory workers, and generate forty-three percent of the manufacturing production (Terrones, 1993). Workers in the smaller enterprises also contribute about ten percent of national GDP (Sánchez Ugarte, 1994). Furthermore, the micro and small businesses have a strong cultural importance, reflecting the importance of the family as the central social unit in Mexico. It will certainly be more effective and expedient to modernize these businesses than it would be to try to alter Mexican culture to value large corporate structures based on shareholder concerns.

The most important characteristics of smaller enterprises are the creation of jobs, contribution to the regional balance of income, provision of components for larger companies, ability to specialize, flexibility to respond to market changes, and rational use of regional resources. They can adapt, innovate, decide and act faster than big companies. Small business can gauge changing consumer behavior to enter new markets untouched by larger companies. In Mexico, larger industries include the automobile, electronics, and appliances industries. These larger industries are serviced by traditional smaller firms in the textile, publishing and printing, food products, shoes, clothing, furniture, leather goods, wood and cork industries, which contribute up to fifty-five percent of the intermediate goods supply. On the other hand, the smaller firms make up only twenty percent of the activities that require high levels of investment in assets and a greater degree of technological development (Terrones, 1993). By modernizing the smaller businesses, the end users can be assured of a supply of quality low-cost components.

On the other hand, the small enterprise has several problems that affect efficiency and advancement. Opportunities to form linkages with larger firms are limited in that only 4 percent of micro firms in Mexico act as direct suppliers for the larger firms (OECD, 1996). Productivity and profitability may be reduced by low skill levels of the labor force, low utilization of installed capacity, lack of technical information for machinery, poor communications, expensive raw material costs as a result of low volume, high credit costs, lack of credit availability, and insufficient size to handle the subcontracting of larger jobs. The resulting squeeze on profit margins usually limits the capacity to save and invest, further reducing any opportunity to adopt new technology (Terrones, 1993).

Some of these problems require better financial support and increased institutional efficiency in the areas of administration, production, commercialization, training, and the quality of the products that must be modernized. The future competitive advantage will be in the technological advances and the creativity to locate and take advantage of the opportunities of open markets, instead of the labor cost and natural resource endowment. In this context it is relevant to foster the growth of investment, technological research and development, the infrastructure, financial support, and training. Two conditions must be met in order to increase the competitive level of the small enterprises. First, the strategy adopted by each company must reflect their planning, administrative processes, suppliers selection, the products that could be produced better, and the channels of commercialization. Second, the characteristics of the environment in which they operate must recognize the state of the infrastructure, efficiency of financing, government regulations, availability of skilled labor and economic stability (Terrones, 1993).

The economic restrictions of the 1980s recession affected small companies in different ways. Moreover, the different strategies used in response to the restrictions made companies more heterogeneous. Three patterns have been identified as to how industries successfully responded to the economic challenge. First, there are industries related to the relatively rapid population growth that survived despite the instability of the market. This was the pattern followed by the greatest number of surviving companies. The second group took advantage of the crisis in the exchange rate to increase their technology and produce items for big enterprises. The third group is composed of companies that were the most dynamic. They were able to enter external markets by exporting directly, or by providing supplies for the exporting companies (Ruiz, 1993). Larger firms, on the other hand, were able to survive through four key strategies. Multinational firms survived the economic crisis by reducing production costs, 27 percent; adopting a new corporate strategy, 16 percent; improving product quality, 15 percent; or exploiting new export opportunities, 12 percent (UNCTC, 1992).

The micro and small companies have had to change from a closed model to an open model in response to the challenge from the developing economies of Asia. The result of this change has been a decreased profit rate due to competition. The number of companies that closed down has increased, specially in industries related to wood, plastics, and textiles. A poll of micro and small enterprises revealed that thirty-eight percent considered that the opening of the economy had reduced their sales; thirty-four percent felt that they had not been affected; twenty-one percent thought that it had been positive in either their sales or technology; and eighty-four percent felt they needed government support to be more competitive (Ruiz, 1993). The overwhelming view that they need government support reflects both limited small firm resources and a cultural preference for government support and leadership of industrial initiatives.

Competition against Asian companies took place in conditions that were very different from those facing the Mexican companies under the closed market conditions of the import substitution policy. Asian companies may receive government support in the form of subsidies; however, small Mexican firms rarely receive direct government support. In another poll it was revealed that forty-seven percent of the owners did not know how international markets worked, which limited their exports; twenty-four percent admitted inadequacies in costs, prices and quality; sixteen percent argued that the local demand did not allow them to export; and five percent said that they needed capital. Ruiz concludes that the companies need to look for strategic associations, to be more open to reorganization of corporate style, and creation of planning associations according to fields or areas. Many Mexican firms continue to believe that additional government support in will be needed to prevent Asian competitors from invading domestic markets, although the NAFTA has already established some barriers against Asian firms (Ruiz, 1993).

In order to break the out of low added value markets, Mexican companies have to adopt technology that will allow them to enter new networks with higher value added. To be able to accomplish that, it has to be understood that the technological potential of micro and small companies can be fundamentally found in the process, and not in the innovation of products. Ruiz notes that this proposition goes against what has been done in developed countries and many emerging economies, including Mexico, where the emphasis has been given to the product and not the process (Ruiz, 1993). Nearly one-half of total R&D activity in the four selected industrial sectors is aimed at the introduction of new products, trailed by efforts to improve quality, improve the process, or improve machinery. Mexican firms must not continue to wait until a producer shows them a new product or prototype. Instead, companies will have to select strategic areas to develop technology, but taking the economic and social structure in the country into consideration to make heterogeneous groups with the purpose of doing research on processes. The revised industrial policy suggests new forms of organization that are becoming farther apart from the traditional vertical model and moving closer to a horizontal model. These new forms of organization and the complementary policies are reflected in the different practices of the case study firms reviewed later in this book. See Figure 7.1.

FIGURE 7.1

REASONS FOR CONDUCTING R&D

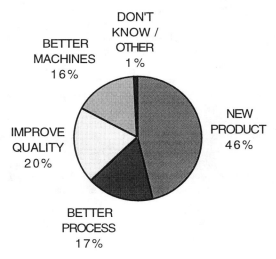

Source: STPS and INEGI, 1995

Multinational firms, through location of operations in a second country or through subcontracting, are able to benefit from the specialized inputs of the rich economy, such as technology, while also benefiting from the input of the poor economy, such as relatively cheap labor (Rodríguez-Clare, 1996). This tendency over time to replace imported components with domestically supplied inputs and processes from subcontractors has been termed "vertical disintegration" (Lim and Fong, 1982). The vertical disintegration will, curiously, aid in the creation of market opportunities for smaller firms.   Flexibility in production will also allow the larger companies to keep their assembling processes, while buying most of the components from the revitalized small enterprises through subcontracting procedures (Ruiz, 1993).

The multinational corporations, in contrast to smaller domestic businesses, have taken the lead in establishing subcontracting arrangements.   Subcontracting is used by approximately sixty percent of multinationals operating in Mexico, according to the UNCTC survey.   All of the subsidiaries in the automotive and computer industries, for example, used subcontracting on an extensive basis to reduce the number of components produced and to reduce costs.   The automobile subsidiaries were obligated by the parent to subcontract some of their production.   The extensive use of subcontracting is beginning to provide backward linkages to small firms in Mexico, particularly through the provision of training for quality control.   The limitations to further use of subcontracting include inadequate quality control, lack of price competitiveness, and use of inadequate technology by the supplier firms (UNCTC, 1992).   As Mexican firms begin to subcontract domestically to a greater extent, it can be assumed that the smaller enterprises will gain through exploitation of new technology and niche market opportunities.

---

[1] In this study, firms with 250 or less employees are characterized as "smaller" firms. The firms in the INEGI/STPS survey were segregated into four groups by size: 2,094 large firms with 251 or more employees; 2,720 medium firms with between 101 and 250 employees; 13,117 small firms with between 16 and 100 employees; and 120,843 micro firms with between 1 and 15 employees.

Chapter 8

The Role of Multinational Corporations and the Maquiladoras

In contrast to most small Mexican firms, the large multinational corporations, or MNCs, typically have access to technology from abroad. The MNCs also play a substantial role in forming the international competitive position of Mexico. Multinational firms control nearly one hundred percent of several of the most important export industries, including automobiles, electronic equipment, and computers. Foreign firms, such as Celanese, Eastman Kodak, and DuPont also control a relatively high 61 percent of the secondary petrochemical industry. The role of the MNCs is particularly important in that their intra-firm exports, led by automobile and engine exports, account for roughly one-third of all Mexican manufactured goods exports (UNCTC, 1992).[1] Principal products of foreign-owned multinational subsidiaries, with foreign ownership in excess of 49 percent, include automobiles and engines, chemicals, computers, and pharmaceuticals. Mixed firms, defined as those with foreign ownership of between 25 and 49 percent, specialize mainly in petrochemicals, auto parts, and cement. As noted previously, most surveys of Mexican industry have not included local firms with less than 25 percent foreign ownership (UNCTC, 1992).

Subsidiaries of multinational corporations usually obtain technology from a foreign supplier, typically the parent corporation. Conversely, the Mexican firms rarely acquire leading technology from their own subsidiaries or related firms. A United Nations survey revealed that the reasons given by Mexican industry executives for acquiring technology include increased competitiveness in the domestic market, increased international competitiveness, and reduced production cost (UNCTC, 1992). It is interesting that the primary reason for technology transfer as surveyed was increased competitiveness in the domestic market. Many Mexican firms look first to compete in the home market, then look to export, in contrast to firms from the export-driven economies. However, many of the MNCs, and in particular the automobile industry, are geared directly for export as a first priority, with the United States serving as the major outlet for production.

It has been stated that multinational corporations, as the major source of technology in the world, make their largest contribution to economic development through the transfer of technology (UNCTC, 1992). Nevertheless, studies of technology transfer by MNCs have not provided a definitive view of the effectiveness of different strategies and organizational structures. According to Rodríguez-Clare (1996), "Multinationals increase world welfare by serving as a channel through which the host country effectively obtains access to resources that are relatively abundant in the home country. Unfortunately, very little is known about how multinationals affect the host country through other important channels, such as the transfer of technology, the training of workers and the generation of linkages." The MNCs have an opportunity to increase the vitality of linkages within Mexico, both for foreign and domestic firms, through technology transfer and training programs.

Backward linkages are developed through the creation of specialized inputs for a final-good firm, creating an externality for other final good producers (Hirschman, 1958). Most linkages created by multinational corporations are backward linkages, since most products are either intermediate goods for use in other good or final goods destined for export (Lim and Fong, 1982). The domestic production of specialized inputs can then be used for production of complex goods, creating forward linkages. The development of effective backward and forward linkages may serve to develop an economy better than the conventional pursuit of balanced growth (Rodríguez-Clare, 1996).

The relative impact of multinational firms on an economy is dependent on the number of linkages created as compared to the domestic linkages displaced by the multinational firms. The multinational firms from further away are relatively more likely to create linkages as a result of higher home to host communication costs, and social, cultural, and legal differences (Rodríguez-Clare, 1996). Further, industries with a relatively high technology base, such as automobiles or electronics, are less likely to provide spillover of technology into other sectors of the economy than are relatively low technology industries. This observation supports increased efforts to increase generic technology capability in low technology industries, such as the apparel industry. Moreover, the greater the degree of embodiment of technology in capital stock, as opposed to human resources, the less the likelihood of spillover effects into other industries (Kokko, 1994). Although government and industrial policy may be aimed at creating linkages between domestic firms, many of the advantages may be lost through creation of leakages, such as an increasing reliance on imports of inputs or the export of intermediate goods. In a worst case scenario, the creation of an export-oriented industrialization may create dependency on the consumer nations (Weisskoff and Wolff, 1977).

In addition, it should be noted that most linkages are created through the direct effort of the industrial sector, not through the efforts of government to stimulate formation of linkages through industrial policy or local content legislation. The establishment of linkages, then, is a distinct concern that must be directly addressed by Mexican firms in concert with multinational corporations. It is not, and cannot be, solely the responsibility of the Mexican government. The linkages should not only be technical in nature, but also embody cooperation in the form of technical assistance, financial aid, managerial advice, and marketing information (Lim and Fong, 1982).

In contrast, industries that exhibit enclave characteristics, or those foreign firms operating in isolation from domestic firms, provide relatively little technology spillover. Further, if the economies of scale that are necessary to compete are very large, the domestic industry is likely to be replaced by the multinational corporations, again reducing the potential for domestic technology transfer (Kokko, 1994). That is, in the industries in which the predominant firms are large foreign multinationals, the opportunity for technology transfer into domestic industry is lessened, although the overall impact is also driven by the host country technology policy. The automobile industry is a clear example of an enclave industry, although there may be a limited number of technology linkages developed through the production of subcontracted auto parts. This is reflected in the slow development of linkages between the automobile producers and the smaller Mexican parts suppliers.

Mexico's common border with the United States provides unique opportunities for industrial cooperation and linkages. Maquiladoras[2], or in-bond plants of multinational corporations, may also play a role in the transfer of technology. Mexican maquiladoras receive goods from the United States, perform a process or assembly operation, and then return the product to the United States. The maquiladoras present a special case through their structure as wholly owned enterprises dedicated to export. In July 1994, there were 2,065 maquiladoras in Mexico employing 579,519 people, with the majority of maquiladoras owned by U.S. firms (Kopinak, 1995). The maquiladoras are the third largest source of foreign exchange in Mexico, following the petroleum and tourism industries. Although the maquiladoras have created jobs and serve as a primary source of foreign exchange, they have been consistently criticized for having limited impact on the industrialization process, technology transfer, or international competitiveness. Further, since between sixty and seventy-five percent of all wages earned by maquiladora workers are subsequently spent in the United States, a leakage exists in the retention of foreign exchange earnings (Grunwald, 1991).

Maquiladora operations may be divided into three categories: assemblers, manufacturers, and advanced technology plants. Assembly plants simply put parts together, while manufacturers use machinery to fabricate product. The traditional assemblers and manufacturers are seen as unable to compete with the flexible production technology in the advanced plants. As such, the advanced technology plants are likely to create more jobs in the future, largely at the expense of assembly and manufacturing plants. The assemblers and manufacturers, on the other hand, will continue to rely on cost advantages, largely through low worker wages and exchange rate differentials (Kopinak, 1995). Many Mexican maquiladoras adopted flexible manufacturing techniques during the 1980s, opening the door to higher value added manufacturing. Productivity changes, coupled with lower real labor wages, have increased the net competitive position of Mexican products as compared to those of other countries. Several academic studies have documented the use of flexible manufacturing techniques in both the Ford Hermosillo plant and automotive maquiladoras (Wilson, 1992).

The maquiladora program, moreover, has been successful in obtaining jobs at the expense of third nations. Prior to the maquiladora program, Hong Kong and Taiwan had the largest shares of overseas end product assembly operations for U.S. firms. Within ten years of the introduction of the maquiladora program, Mexico had more than twice the share of Hong Kong and four times the share of Taiwan. In many cases, the proximity of the Mexican market to the other NAFTA markets is sufficient to lower transportation costs far enough to overcome potential wage advantages of Southeast Asian assemblers (Grunwald and Flamm, 1985).

The original charter of the maquiladora program specifically included transfer of technology from the parent multinational corporation, which "promote investment in advanced technology sectors, and incorporate new technology which modernizes production processes." Unfortunately, in many cases little technology transfer has actually been accomplished. Until recently, multinational corporations have routinely been accused of rarely transferred technology until it has become obsolete (Sklair, 1993). However, recent studies have led some researchers to note that for the best maquiladoras the practices are similar to those used in the parent firm (Sargent and Matthews, 1997). Further, it has been written that little has been done to increase the knowledge base of the Mexican employee as related to design or processes, with most of the technology transfer taking the form of training of Mexican managers in techniques for control of production flows (Grunwald, 1991). The Japanese maquiladoras train at somewhat higher levels than the U.S. maquiladoras, with the Mexican maquiladoras lagging far behind. However, none of the maquiladora operations exhibit training levels comparable to those found at the parent operations (Raafat, 1992). It is likely that some, if not most, of the rhetoric on the relative age of the technology transferred to Mexico is correct. Much of the technology is obsolete, at least by U.S. standards. However, it is quite likely that much of this technology is appropriate for the current state of Mexican manufacturing.

In general, the maquiladoras cannot or do not produce products other than for the parent company; however, they provide a very positive aspect in the substantial employment opportunities and basic training offered. Further, inputs are most always imported. The maquiladoras consumed over \$10 billion of components in 1989, but less than two percent were of Mexican origin (Grunwald, 1991). As such, the maquiladoras are participating in technology relocation from a plant located in the United States, and owing to their proximity to the United States contribute relatively few technology linkages (Rodríguez-Clare, 1996).[3] This may, however, be changing. Maquiladoras located in the interior of the country typically create more input backward linkages by buying from domestic suppliers than do the maquiladoras near the border. Nearly twenty percent of all maquiladoras are now in the interior of the country, as compared to less than ten percent in 1975 (Wilson, 1992). Nonetheless, the maquiladoras have been characterized as an enclave industry for several reasons. These include not only the low percentage of Mexican materials used in production, but also the employment of young women instead of traditional unemployed groups, concentration along the border, reliance on relatively unskilled labor, little transfer of technology beyond production management techniques, and low wages and benefits (Grunwald and Flamm, 1985).

The maquiladora industry has been characterized as an example of fragmentary export industrialization growth. In general, maquiladoras do not develop products, conduct research and development, or substantially upgrade human resources. They do not develop very much hard technology, such as equipment and machinery, nor do they develop soft technology, such as innovative methods for the organization of work. The private sector does not invest heavily in technology for maquiladoras, preferring to use them as low-cost production sites. More importantly, the Mexican government has not been able to find a way to facilitate the introduction of technology into the maquiladoras nor to transfer technology from the maquiladoras to the private sector (Kopinak, 1995). Nonetheless, the maquiladora program has been an important part of the Mexican economic development. The program has provided jobs with good pay, and further has provided a basic level of training to many workers who otherwise would have been unemployed or underemployed.

Unlike technology relocation, technology transfer requires anchorage to achieve a permanent state of information flow. That is, the technology must be able to be used other than for the specific task assigned by the parent. For most maquiladoras, the technology imported is not expected to find applications beyond the primary product, and workers are not trained or expected to apply the technology to other areas. This was particularly the case for the first maquiladoras, which produced low technology goods such as apparel, gloves, toys, and dolls. More recently, three-quarters of all maquiladora production is composed of high technology goods, such as automobiles, auto parts, televisions, semiconductors, and office machines. This shift in the nature of the goods produced has been accompanied by an increase in the intensity of technology transfer (Grunwald, 1991). As a consequence, the multinationals have begun to address the technology deficit problem by mixing high technology manufacturing with low wage labor. Examples of multinationals now increasing the level and quality of technology transfer include Allied Bendix, Ford, Unisys, and Eastman Kodak (Sklair, 1993).

A key difficulty in the upgrading of worker technical skill at the maquiladora operations lies in the high turnover rate of personnel, which in many cases reaches levels of over one hundred percent per year. Salary is one of the key factors in encouraging the relocation of employees between firms, although there are many other complicating factors in the personnel turnover problem.   The Mexican worker's salary, in real terms, fell by more than 25 percent between 1980 and 1988.   The workers had returned to 90 percent of their prior real wages by 1994, but the devaluation and ensuing inflation has again greatly reduced the purchasing power of nearly all workers.   Other retention difficulties stem from the relatively young age of the workers and the competitive market that bids workers away from other firms for relatively small changes in wages and benefits.

---

[1]Note that the United States provides statistics for intra-firm exports separately from other export statistics.   Mexico, like many other countries, does not make this distinction.   As a result, the percentages reported for intra-firm exports are estimates.

[2]Grunwald provides a clear description of the regulations supporting U.S. customs regulations 806 and 807.   The maquiladora program, formally known as the Mexican Border Industrialization Program, was initiated in 1965.   The program takes advantage of U.S. tariff schedules 806 and 807 for the final assembly of goods.   Imports under sections 806 and 807 are reported to account for more than ten percent of the value of all U.S. merchandise imports.   Maquiladoras are often referred to as twin plants, an idea under which the U.S. plant adds capital-intensive production and the Mexican plant provides labor-intensive production.   In reality, very few twin plants exist as most U.S. plants doing business with maquiladoras are located in the Midwest states.   The greatest number of maquiladoras are located in Tijuana, Mexicali, Nogales, Agua Prieta, Ciudad Juárez, Matamoros, and other cities along the border (Grunwald and Flamm, 1985).

[3]The Mexican government initially agreed to the maquiladora program with the provision that all maquiladoras be located within twenty kilometers of the border.   Although maquiladoras are now located throughout Mexico, more than ninety percent of all maquiladoras continue to be located near the border (Grunwald and Flamm, 1985).

Chapter 9

The Role of Training Programs

In any modern economy, worker training has become equally important with traditional educational programs. Education and training are viewed as vital components in establishing and sustaining national competitive advantage (Porter, 1990). Economies that develop and sustain economic leadership have achieved not only the required micro-level investment in workers through training, but have also created a macro-level training infrastructure through both cultural change and governmental policy and support (Warner, 1994). Unfortunately, the emphasis on formal training programs is a relatively new phenomenon in Mexico. All Mexican companies are required by law to provide job training to their employees; however, it is estimated that only about thirty-six percent of companies comply with this regulation. In an effort to catch up, the market for training services grew seventy percent between 1991 and 1993, and is expected to continue to grow in excess of ten percent per year as Mexican industry seeks to modernize (Herrera, 1993).

Although some Mexican firms have been conducting training programs for years, the relatively small size of the average firm, the lack of capital for uninterrupted training programs, and the past protection of the domestic market have hindered the creation of a management culture which values training programs. As a result, most training programs are of short duration and do not have the resources necessary to effectively improve worker skills. The STPS-INEGI study concluded that 18.48 percent of the Mexican employed labor force had taken training courses, although 6.56 percent had taken more than five hundred training hours (STPS and INEGI, 1995). In the United States, more than one out of every four workers had the same level of training (Herrera, 1993).

The Mexican government is also cooperating in the drive to increase the overall training level for industry personnel. CONACYT has enrolled more industry personnel in training programs as a means of expanding the technological base. This effort has met with some success. By 1994, the CONACYT training programs enrolled 14,250 students, a significant increase from the 2,235 students in 1988. Further expansion of these programs will play a significant role in diversifying the resources available for technological development. Nevertheless, Mexican training programs sponsored by the government fell far short of those in comparable nations. For example, South Korea enrolls more than fifty thousand trainees in programs per year (Greene, 1994).

Government and industry have also cooperated to develop vocational training programs. Vocational training is largely provided through Ministry of Education programs in the public sector; however, the number of private training programs is rising rapidly. Cooperation between industry, government, and educational institutions in the establishment of training centers has been rising rapidly with team efforts to identify specific training needs and in the development of curriculum plans. Some of the training centers have been linked directly to local industry, both through instructional input and provision of scholarships. Most of the training centers have been established by joint ventures of the largest companies. The trade ministry and the national chamber of manufacturers, known as CANACINTRA, sponsor joint programs to transfer technology from research centers to industry (OECD, 1996). If the training center concept is to reach its potential, smaller companies will need to be included in the planning and implementation process. The potential for the growth of linkages through the training programs cannot be underestimated.

Internally, training programs for current employees are used by most of the larger manufacturers in Mexico; however, the smaller firms offer relatively little formal training. In the textile sector, which is dominated by micro businesses, less than twenty percent of all employees are trained. The high level of training in the large and medium firms is most likely a reflection of the presence of multinational firms and the greater amount of financial resources available for training. Many Mexican firms, especially the small entrepreneurial companies, are looking to use increased levels of managerial training to rapidly increase overall labor capability (Sanchez, 1993). This trend may be able to make a vital difference in the competitive posture of Mexico as it changes the ratio of skilled to unskilled laborers. In many cases, the absence of skilled labor in Mexico leads to a narrowing of employment opportunities for unskilled labor (Alarcon and McKinley, 1997). As can be seen in TABLE 9.1, levels of training vary widely by industry and by size of the firm.

TABLE 9.1

COMPANIES THAT OFFER TRAINING PROGRAMS
TO ALL EMPLOYEES, PERCENT

	Total	Large	Medium	Small	Micro
Textiles	18.2	81.1	66.4	42.6	9.0
Chemicals	56.9	92.9	81.2	65.1	42.8
Metals	38.9	92.8	77.0	43.1	21.5
Automobile	48.7	96.1	77.5	64.0	17.5

Source: STPS and INEGI, 1995

Many Mexican firms are growing in sales and number of personnel employed and are only recently beginning to realize the advantages of formal training programs. Some industries, such as the automobile industry, are using training of new employees as an alternative to hiring experienced workers, providing a younger work force with less bad habits or union influence. The older worker is replaced with a younger worker as essentially an interchangeable part. In addition, the requirement of higher quality production to compete with imported products is forcing many firms to use training as a means of improving product quality.

The amount of training reported for new employees is much higher than that of current employees. This, in part, reflects the young age of most new employees in Mexico and dissatisfaction with the formal education system, which continues to fail to provide sufficient quantities of workers ready to adapt to new production methods and work organization. The micro industries show the largest increase, with between twenty and sixty percent of the number of new employees receiving formal training. Each of the four industries studied reports training for more than seventy percent of the new hires. This reflects, in part, the novelty of using training in Mexico. See TABLE 9.2.

TABLE 9.2

COMPANIES OFFERING TRAINING PROGRAMS
TO NEW EMPLOYEES, PERCENT

	Total	Large	Medium	Small	Micro
Textiles	77.7	86.2	79.1	82.0	70.8
Chemicals	72.2	88.5	83.5	72.7	63.9
Metals	73.3	84.4	66.7	89.0	49.0
Automobile	78.2	91.0	77.4	80.5	50.7

Source: STPS and INEGI, 1995

A substantial proportion of training resources are used to hire external trainers. Each of the four selected industry segments reports a relatively high amount of external training, usually by consultants. Since the majority of firms are relatively small, they do not typically have the staff or resources needed to employ professionals in-house to provide training. Further, the great majority of academics in Mexico teach on a part time basis, creating a large supply of potential consultants at reasonable cost. In the state public universities, for example, less than thirty percent of all faculty were full time employees in 1993 (Barros Valero, 1994). As such, the use of consultants from academia is popular with many industrial firms.

Unfortunately, the relatively low level of demand for technical support services has continued to slow creation of firms that directly serve the business community (Camacho, 1994). In many areas, this vital service is almost totally absent, retarding growth of smaller firms that lack the ability to provide their own support services. Larger firms tend to take advantage of support services much more often than do the smaller firms, which lack both financial resources and a management culture which values the use of training programs. For example, the metals industry, which has been largely privatized and enjoys several joint ventures with multinational firms, has the highest rate of use of external trainers. The foreign ownership of the automobile producers indicates a trend toward a higher use of in-house specialists from the parent company's home operations. In any event, it appears that a higher level of outside contact, whether by ownership or strategic alliance, increases the likelihood that a firm will seek out external help in training employees or will set up its own training program. In this light, the continued trend toward increased foreign investment and joint ventures will not only benefit those companies participating directly, but will also provide opportunities for smaller firms to benefit from the establishment of local training firms and consulting businesses. See TABLE 9.3.

TABLE 9.3

FIRMS THAT USE EXTERNAL TRAINERS
PERCENT

Textiles	48.1
Chemicals	59.5
Metals	79.3
Automobile	59.0

Source: STPS and INEGI, 1995

Introduction of new equipment is typically used to provide increased product quality or to increase production quantity, and in many countries is used to reduce the need for high wage labor. As would be expected, Mexican firms, in general, do not report widespread use of machinery to replace relatively low wage workers. Only six percent of new equipment recently installed has resulted in a reported decrease in employment, while forty-five percent of firms reported increased employment with the introduction of new equipment. New equipment, then, is used primarily to increase the quality and quantity of output of a firm rather than simply to defend domestic market share.

This appears to support the commonly held concept that Mexico has a large excess labor supply that might be more highly productive with the introduction of new capital technology and machinery, leading to improved supply of higher quality goods into both the domestic and export markets. This viewpoint is reinforced by the emphasis given to the development of a modern industrial sector in the government's recent economic plans, and in particular the emphasis given to the development of a strong export capacity in the automotive and steel sectors. Clearly, the use of newer equipment in the leading sectors is seen as a way to improve competitiveness not only in the export market, but also in the domestic market against low-cost or high-quality foreign competitors. The trend toward use of more new equipment, and less used or obsolete equipment, is likely to continue. See Figure 9.1.

FIGURE 9.1

EFFECT OF EQUIPMENT ON EMPLOYMENT

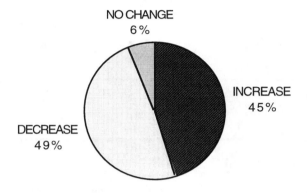

Source: STPS and INEGI, 1995

The introduction of new equipment has increased the knowledge needs of the Mexican worker. Of the Mexican firms surveyed, fifty-three percent reported an increased need for worker training and the other forty-seven percent reported no change in the knowledge needs. None of the firms reported that use of new equipment would reduce the need for training. This result is consistent with other studies in which the introduction of integrated manufacturing did not require increased training for most workers, and that introduction of new equipment may even lead to the "deskilling" of workers in that many jobs will be simplified and streamlined (Sargent and Matthews, 1997). The relatively low positive response, when contrasted with the very low levels of training currently in use by some industry segments, reveals that many businesses do not yet understand the importance of training programs in the development of employee capabilities and productivity. Unfortunately, many firms that do want to introduce additional training programs are unable to do so because of the economic constraints of the recession and uncertainty about future economic performance, especially in light of the series of three severe economic crises related to the value of the peso. Apparently, the increased use of modern equipment and manufacturing methods in a modern industrial sector in Mexico will require more extensive training programs by firms, eventually leading to increased management appreciation of the importance of training programs. Worker training remains a key component toward realizing a sustained drive toward industrial competitiveness for Mexican manufacturers. See Figure 9.2.

FIGURE 9.2

EFFECT OF NEW EQUIPMENT ON WORKER KNOWLEDGE NEEDS

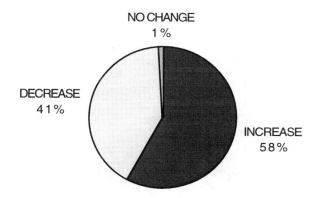

Source: INEGI

The use of quality control methods, and in some cases the lack of quality control methods, also reflects the future need for increased adoption of international practices for competition in the open market. Quality control, much the same as other traditional training areas, appears to be a relatively new idea in Mexico. This reflects the traditional Mexican culture of buying on price first, without regard to product quality. Relatively low product quality remains a concern, with the textile and metals industries spending over four percent of income on replacement of defective products (STPS and INEGI, 1995). Roughly three out of every four Mexican manufacturing firms report use of quality control techniques, while less than twenty percent do not use any quality control methods. As competition increases from international firms, it is quite likely that nearly all Mexican firms will be forced to employ quality control in the production of goods.

In addition, quality control procedures are in the future likely to employ more statistical methodology as opposed to simple visual or mechanical quality checks. Currently, ninety percent of firms use only visual quality control methods, especially in the relatively low-technology textile industry. The segments of industry that compete in the world market, such as automobiles and steel, are much more likely to have adopted statistical processes. Again, the change toward modernized methods is likely to be slow and to continue along a firm by firm and industry by industry path as foreign competition forces companies to produce higher quality goods or lose their markets. Mexican firms will need to actively pursue benchmarking programs in order to develop quality control procedures that match the needs of the international markets. See Figure 9.3.

FIGURE 9.3

PERCENTAGE OF FIRMS USING QUALITY CONTROL

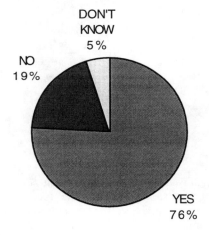

Source: STPS and INEGI, 1995

Chapter 10

Mexican Manufacturing and Industrial Competitiveness

The manufacturing sector is key to providing new jobs for the growing Mexican population. From 1970 to 1990, the employment growth in Mexico was lower than the number of Economically Active People, or PEA.[1] The PEA grows by 1.2 million people each year, requiring an increase of five percent in the number of available jobs just to keep even. The Mexican economy should increase its formal jobs by at least that percentage in order to satisfy the minimum needs of labor by the Mexican society. The difference approaches 385 thousand jobs annually, with the gap growing wider in recent years.

As the rate of unemployment and underemployment has grown, subcontracting and the participation in the informal sector, or underground economy, has also grown. None of the major manufacturing groups has consistently recorded an annual growth rate of five percent. Only two employment groups, automobile production and fruit and vegetable production, have generated employment growth near five percent per year. These two groups, unfortunately, only have a small percentage in total employment. The automobile sector is, however, capable of creating opportunities for companies in other sectors to act as suppliers, and as such can act as a catalyst to create jobs for smaller firms. The lack of leading sectors that can dynamically create jobs has resulted in slow job growth in many sectors that were expected to flourish following the NAFTA. Unfortunately, one of the principal characteristics of the Mexican economy following trade liberalization has been the growing trend of excluding large numbers of people that are trying to join the formal economy, swelling the ranks of unemployed and underemployed workers and those joining the underground economy (Dussel, 1995).

The manufacturing sector, which acts as the gate into increased technical capacity and capability, has a limited but growing role in the Mexican economy. Since 1980, its participation in the GNP has been around twenty-one percent of all output and twelve percent in total employment (Dussel, 1995). The supply of manufactured goods to the Mexican industrial and consumer markets is overwhelmingly filled by Mexican and U.S. producers, with nearly ninety-three percent of the market (Wylie, 1995). This pattern is reflective of the consumption patterns of the other NAFTA trading partners.

The United States supplies 72.1 percent of all of Mexico's imported manufactures, followed by the European Community at 12.6 percent. Under the NAFTA, Mexican manufacturing will rely even more heavily on the importation of products from the United States and Canada, supplanting about 9 percent of imports from other nations outside the NAFTA. The European Community and Japan will both lose approximately nine percent of their trade with Mexico. Contrary to popular belief, Mexico's trade pattern is increasingly becoming more regional in nature and less connected to the global trading system. This regionalization effect will be strongest for the plastics, apparel, fabricated metal products, and transportation equipment sectors (Wylie, 1995). In general, the three NAFTA partners prefer to trade first among themselves, and then with European or Asian nations. The arrangement increasingly has the United States as the hub for all trade, and the NAFTA has failed to significantly increase trade between Mexico and Canada.

The development of the Mexican economy will rely on increased availability of manufacturing jobs, providing a springboard for quality jobs created through the specialization of labor and demand for a wider variety of products. Unfortunately, bottlenecks in the production process, usually resulting from technology and equipment problems, have reduced the ability of Mexican manufacturers to produce quality goods at competitive costs, resulting in lost opportunities for increased penetration of international markets (Olmedo, 1996). For example, the textile industry lacks sufficient capacity in the dyeing and finishing areas and is unable to convert domestic cloth in sufficient quantity to supply the growing apparel industry. Imported cloth reduces the potential cost advantages of the apparel sector, inhibiting growth in that industry segment. As Mexico looks to modernize, key production sectors will need to be identified and developed to provide linkages into secondary sectors.

Much of the new manufacturing emphasis is keyed to the development of an efficient exporting industry. The automobile industry has grown with a stated goal of exporting, but the other three selected industries continue to sell primarily to the domestic market. Sales of the four selected sectors by country are summarized in TABLE 10.1.

TABLE 10.1

SALES BY SECTOR AND COUNTRY OF DESTINATION,
PERCENT, 1991

	Mexico	USA	Canada	Others
Textiles	83.7	10.4	0.5	5.3
Chemicals	89.5	3.7	0.1	6.6
Metals	80.7	9.3	0.1	9.9
Automobile	57.6	36.4	3.4	3.7

Source: INEGI and STPS, 1995

It is useful to examine the development of the manufacturing sector by areas. According to the National System of Accounts, a branch of INEGI, there are forty-nine industrial groups divided into three groups based on the average growth annual rate. First group industries are characterized by a range of their average growth annual rates from 2.0 percent to 4.9 percent, second group industries have a range of about two percent, and the third sector has a rate lower than two percent. The 16 areas of the first group, especially the first five industries (automobiles, basic petrochemicals, beer, glass and glass products, and electronic apparatus), represent the leading areas of the manufacturing sector with a greater potential to achieve modernization and a successful integration in the world market. These areas are, in general, related to multinational corporations, monopolies, or national oligopolies. Consequently, they are also the areas of production that have the highest level of access to international capital sources and modern, appropriate technology. In contrast, industrial sectors in the third group are typically the traditional industries, such as food, tobacco, textiles, leather and shoes. Many of these industries are large employers, but they have growth rates that are typically only one-fifth those of the leading industrial sectors. Over the long term, these industries are likely to feel the most pressure from imports from other emerging economies, and in many cases will find it difficult to maintain present employment levels, let alone create new jobs (Dussel, 1995).

Dussel's classification of industries shows that the most dynamic areas, since the beginning of the liberalization strategy, have been dominated by multinational corporations, national monopolies, or oligopolies (Dussel, 1995). Indeed, the development of the Mexican economy is likely to become more dependent on foreign firms, rather than less. Nonetheless, both international and domestic cooperation will be required to succeed in the creation of a sustainable technology development process. According to Patel, "Expecting that the private sector and particularly transnational enterprises will build in Mexico something close to a self-reliant scientific and technological capability amounts to believing in miracles. These two considerations seem to suggest that the future of technological transformation in Mexico is very bleak indeed." (Patel, 1993). It can be concluded that Mexico's revised technology policies, which blend domestic and imported technology, are more likely to succeed than were the import substitution policies. The revised policies, needless to say, will be much more favorable toward foreign firms operating in Mexico than were the earlier policies.

There are, however, some very promising aspects of recent industry efforts to increase Mexico's domestically created technology aimed at improving manufacturing competitiveness. The increased level of international competition resulting from the opening of the market and the NAFTA has spurred concerted efforts to upgrade manufacturing capability. The U.S. International Trade Commission expects to see increases in machine exports from the United States to Mexico as a result of NAFTA, although Mexico is unlikely to increase machine exports to the United States by any significant amount (Weintraub, 1992). The improved opportunity to receive new equipment should generally strengthen Mexico's competitive position as compared to third countries.

Mexican firms are responding to the increased openness of the domestic industrial and consumer markets. In the INEGI-STPS survey, over one-half of the firms surveyed reported strong competition from imported products, and only fifteen percent perceived competition from imports as being weak. Relatively few firms, twenty-one percent, have not felt the influence of the open market. It appears that many domestic firms are increasingly concerned about imported goods and their ability to compete on quality and cost. This represents a substantial change from the historical view of competition based primarily on the selling price of the good, without any concern for product quality or other service to the consumer. Product price is rapidly being supplanted by the value of the product, both in the domestic and international markets. See Figure 10.1.

FIGURE 10.1

DEGREE OF COMPETITION FROM IMPORTED PRODUCTS

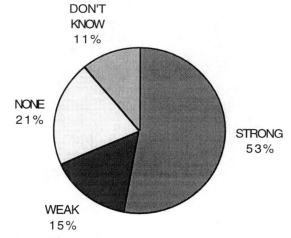

Source: STPS and INEGI, 1995

The manufacturing sector has continued to move forward somewhat steadily in spite of the peso devaluation. Contrary to popular belief, the upgrading of manufacturing equipment has continued throughout the difficult period of economic recovery, particularly in the critical steel and automobile sectors. Not only are the multinational corporations continuing to invest, domestic firms are also taking a longer term approach to installation of new technology and equipment. As a result, many Mexican firms are installing new equipment embodying recent technology, with approximately sixty-eight percent of recent investments going toward new equipment and an additional ten percent toward a mix of new and used equipment. Only twenty-two percent of the firms surveyed reported installation consisting entirely of used equipment. Again, this recent trend toward the use of new equipment indicates that Mexican firms are taking a long-term approach to addressing current and anticipated deficiencies in the capital stock. See Figure 10.2.

FIGURE 10.2

TYPE OF EQUIPMENT INSTALLED

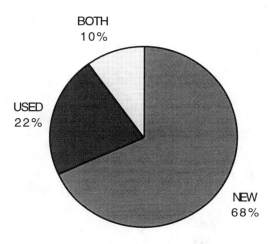

Source: STPS and INEGI, 1995

In each of the four major industries studied, the number of new processes is dwarfed by the mature or updated "newer" processes. The petrochemical, metals, and automobile industries use slightly more mature technology than "newer" technology, while the textile industry uses slightly more "newer" technology than mature technology. It is typical in Mexico, as in many nations, that new processes are only introduced with a new product, and that the introduction of completely new processes are thus very rare events for most sectors of Mexican industry. As stated above, the continuous adoption of new processes without the introduction of complementary new products is required for an updating of Mexican manufacturing technology to global standards. It is quite unlikely that Mexico can continue the same pattern of joint process and product development without falling even further behind her major competitors. See Figure 10.3.

The capital equipment infrastructure adds approximately fifty to sixty percent of the value added in the manufacturing sector (STPS and INEGI, 1995). Mexico's capital stock will require massive investment and updating to approach quality levels comparable to those in the more advanced nations. For example machine tools, at thirty-three percent, and numerical controls, at twenty-nine percent, dominate the machinery used across all four industrial sectors. Use of numerical control equipment, at seven percent of all equipment, and computer controlled equipment, at four percent, is very low by modern industrial standards. Nonetheless, substantial progress is being made in some areas. For example, the use of computer systems in Mexico continues to grow. In 1990, there was one computer for every 116 Mexican citizens. By 1992, the ratio had improved to one computer for every 65 Mexican citizens (Alvarez, 1994). By 1996, there was one computer for every 35 Mexicans, the highest rate of computer availability in Latin America. By 1997, Mexico had 3.72 Internet hosts per 10 thousand people, trailing both Argentina and Brazil (World Bank, 1998). The introduction of the robot into manufacturing, on the other hand, appears to remain in the distant future for most Mexican manufacturers. Although some robots are currently used in Mexico, each of the four industries in this study reports an average of zero robots across the plants surveyed, with the automobile industry reporting some use of robots (STPS and INEGI, 1995).

FIGURE 10.3

ESTABLISHMENTS BY TYPE OF PROCESS

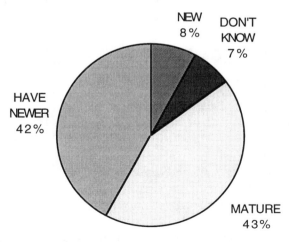

Source: STPS and INEGI, 1995

Machine tools and manual equipment dominate each of the four industries studied. Automobile manufacturers reported the greatest use of machines per factory, with nearly fifty machine tools and forty-five pieces of manual equipment. The level of equipment used falls off rapidly for the metals, chemicals, and textile sectors. The value of machinery in the chemical industry is led by automatic equipment. In the textile, chemical, and automobile industries the value of machine tools dominates the other type of equipment. Relatively low levels of numerical control machines, computer control machines, and robots are used by any of the industries. Reluctance to install relatively high technology machinery may prove to be especially troublesome in the long run as Mexican firms fall further behind on a long learning curve. In particular, successful implementation of newer technology by small and medium businesses will need to follow the lead of larger businesses (Ebel, 1991).

TABLE 10.4

AVERAGE NUMBER OF MACHINES BY TYPE AND INDUSTRY

	Textile	Chemicals	Metals	Auto
Total	28	44	85	145
Machine Tools	12	13	27	48
Numerical Control	1	2	8	9
Computer Control	0	1	1	10
Robots	0	0	0	0
Manual Equipment	11	15	18	44
Automatic Equipment	2	7	18	21
Other Equipment	1	6	13	13

Source: STPS and INEGI, 1995

The equipment tends to be used until it wears out, as indicated by the survey result that nearly three-quarters of the firms surveyed had not installed any new equipment between 1989 and 1992. However, the overall result is greatly influenced by the textile sector, which had very little new equipment installed. Over one-half of the chemical and metals firms had installed new equipment, and over two-thirds of the automotive firms had installed new equipment. This indicates that the industries that are installing new technology may have a much better chance of facing global competition than do those industries that are unable to afford new equipment. See Figure 10.4.

FIGURE 10.4

COMPANIES THAT INTRODUCED NEW EQUIPMENT
1989 - 1992

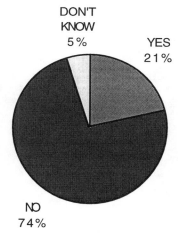

DON'T
KNOW
5%

YES
21%

NO
74%

Source: STPS and INEGI, 1995

[1]The number of economically active people in Mexico is preferred as a measure of employment activity to the conventional unemployment rate. The Mexican government counts as employed any person over twelve years of age who works one or more hours per week, and includes begging as a form of employment. Obviously, this distorts reality dramatically when the PEA is used as the equivalent of the unemployment rate by foreign observers. Rates of between two and five percent are often reported, but most observers assume that the real unemployment and underemployment rate lies between twenty and fifty percent. Canada also uses one hour per week as the standard for employment, and the United States uses fifteen hours per week. For a more complete analysis, see Vicario and Steinberg, 1997.

Chapter 11

Case Study: The Mexican Textile and Apparel Industry

The Mexican textile and apparel industry contributes nine percent of the manufacturing sector's GDP, but perhaps more importantly employs more than 350 thousand Mexican citizens.[1] Apparel manufacturing, which employs the majority of workers in the combined industry, contributes forty-two percent of the total value added by the textile and apparel industry (INEGI, 1995). Nearly one out of every eight jobs in the Mexican manufacturing sector can be attributed to textiles and apparel. As such, the ability to continue to create jobs in this industry is critical to the continued growth and stability of the Mexican economy. The textile industry is concentrated near the center of the country, but apparel manufacturing is scattered across the country.

The industry is dualistic in nature, with relatively larger firms dominating the textile sector and small, cottage industry prevalent in the apparel sector. Further, the industry has faced very rapid change following the passage of the North American Free Trade Agreement. In general, the NAFTA appears to have had an overall positive effect on the Mexican textile and apparel industry, increasing exports, employment, and technological capacity. In this chapter, the influence of technology on the competitiveness of the Mexican and US textile and apparel industries is examined. This appears to be an appropriate form of analysis as 75 percent of Mexican textile exports and 98 percent of apparel exports are destined for the US market. Indeed, following the NAFTA Mexico not only surpassed Canada as the largest exporter of textiles and apparel to the United States, but appears to be drawing market a small amount of market share away from third country competitors (Manzanella, 1996). The highly bilateral trade structure appears to be linked directly to Mexico's recently improved trade position in both the textile and apparel areas.

There are six primary end uses for textiles: clothing, household uses, carpets, industrial applications, tire manufacturing, and miscellaneous uses. Mexico's consumption patterns follow those in the more advanced nations, although Mexico uses over 60 percent synthetic fibers, which is unusually high. This is explained by the proximity to the United States, production of synthetic polymers in Mexico, and disparities in the per capita income. Cotton, polyester, and acrylics are the most utilized fibers (Botella et al, 1991).

The textile industry uses five distinct manufacturing processes, each of which adds substantial value added to the final product. Fiber production, spinning, and fabric finishing each contribute approximately fifteen percent of value added. Fabric manufacturing contributes twenty percent of value added, and cloth manufacturing contributes thirty-five percent of value added (Botella et al, 1991). This has encouraged the development of a high level of vertical integration by Mexican firms, often from the spinning of fibers up to the production of clothing. The largest firms, such as Kaltex and Grupo Saba, are internationally competitive. The Mexican textile industry is substantially more vertically integrated than the industry in other parts of the world.

In some cases, this high level of vertical integration has led to underutilization and bottlenecks in the production process. A recent economic study indicates that Mexican textile mills register only about one-half the productivity of German, Japanese, and US mills. Machinery, technology, training, and basic quality are approximately equal in the four countries. The productivity difference appears to lie in lower utilization of installed capacity, including machine downtime, and relatively short operating times (Botella et al, 1991).

In some cases, the textile firms have begun to buy apparel manufacturers. However, the majority of apparel manufacturing continues to be in the hands of micro (up to 15 employees) and small firms (16 to 100 employees). Only five percent of apparel firms qualify as medium (101 to 250 employees) or large (more than 250 employees). TABLE 11.1, below, summarizes the size of Mexican apparel firms (STPS and INEGI, 1995). The Mexican clothing and apparel sector is notably different from the production of raw fabric in that the great majority of firms are very small, with more than thirty percent of the firms employing less than ten employees and the great majority of firms employing less than fifty employees (Salinas, 1992). Further, seventeen percent of the firms in the sector report that they are in a declining market position, with many small firms threatened by increased domestic and international competition (STPS and INEGI, 1995). Many of the small and micro firms with go out of business, merge, or be bought by the larger, more efficient firms.

The Mexican textile industry contributes two percent of national GDP, with the clothing manufacturing industry contributing about 38.5 percent of all output of the textile and apparel sector in 1994. The sector is a major source of employment in Mexico, creating more than 345 thousand jobs in 1994, out of a total of 2.3 million in the entire manufacturing sector (INEGI, 1995). Some authors report an even larger size for the textile sector. Botella, for example, estimates textile employment at approximately 770 thousand people in Mexico; 35 thousand of these jobs are in the maquiladora sector. Approximately three out of every four textile and apparel jobs are provided by the clothing sector (Botella et al, 1991). Unlike the textile production sector, the apparel sector is among the lowest sectors in capital intensity measured by physical capital per worker (Cline, 1990).

TABLE 11.1

Size of Mexican Apparel Firms, 1995

Company Size	Number of Companies	Percent of Total
Micro	7,731	84.9
Small	1,089	12.0
Medium	187	2.1
Large	93	1.0

Source: STPS and INEGI, 1995

Two technological shifts have dramatically impacted the global textile and apparel industry. First, the introduction of synthetic fibers has altered the inputs of the industry. For example, from 1960 to 1979 the share of synthetic fibers in the industry rose from five percent to thirty-six percent. The highly state-controlled petrochemical industry serves as the raw material provider for much of Mexico's fiber and textile industry, increasing the reliance on synthetic materials as an input to the textile industry. Petrochemical industry capacity utilization in Mexico has remained relatively high despite the recent recession, at approximately seventy-five percent of total capacity. Despite running close to capacity, the Mexican suppliers are not always able to supply key production inputs. This often leads to a need to import raw materials. For example, many Mexican firms have trade contacts with US firms to supply petrochemical raw materials, particularly acrylonitrile, paraxylene, and cyclohexane. Over 50 percent of the acrylonitrile used by the Mexican textile industry is imported from the United States.

Second, use of machinery to replace workers has reduced labor costs and improved competitiveness worldwide (Cline, 1990). More than twenty percent of Mexican textile firms reported installing new equipment between 1989 and 1992 (STPS and INEGI, 1995). The recent trend toward consolidation, foreign investment, and joint ventures will further increase the level of investment in new equipment. Mexican technology for manufacturing is at a world class level for production of manmade fibers, weaving and knitting, cotton processing machinery, and carpets. The weakest link is in the dyeing and finishing sector, leading to high levels of exports for intermediate products. Printing equipment is relatively new, but can only handle about 20 percent of national output (Botella et al, 1991). The great majority of textile machinery used in Mexico is imported from the European Community -- Italy, Germany, Switzerland, France, and Spain -- with the United States and Asia lagging far behind (Salinas, 1992; STPS and INEGI, 1995).

Five major problems have been identified in the technology development of the textile sector in Mexico. First, there is little interaction between higher educational institutions or training centers with the textile industry, with less than four percent of textile firms reporting sharing in the research and development of higher education institutions. Not only are most of the businesses micro or small in size, reducing interaction with higher education, but they are also often located away from Mexico City. Second, there are very few agreements for access to technical assistance with other countries. Since most equipment suppliers are located in Europe, the NAFTA has done little to address this problem. Third, most of the producing micro and small firms do not have sufficient access to equipment modernization funds from commercial banks or government agencies. Noting that of 1,200 domestic suppliers of textiles, only five percent are medium to large firms employing over one hundred workers, it can be directly ascertained that this is a severe problem for the industry. Consequently, only about three percent of Mexican textile firms buy technology and only about twenty percent can afford to buy any new machinery.   This problem has been slightly alleviated during the past four years. Since 1994, spending for plant modernization has risen from 260 million dollars to 360 million dollars. Nonetheless, Mexican plants continue to employ older and less efficient machinery than do their US counterparts. Fourth, little patented technology is diffused throughout the textile sector, and very little new technology for application to textile manufacturing is developed Mexico. Again, the outlook may be changing.   Mexican firms are increasingly seeking and finding investment from abroad, either from the United States or the Far East. With that investment has come not only financial capital, but newer technology (Sutter, 1997). Fifth, the pirating of trademarks and patents reduces the incentive to innovate or to invest in technological development and design (Salinas, 1992; STPS and INEGI, 1995).

In addition, some sectors that impact the textile industry continue to experience severe bottlenecks, indicating that production will fall far short of domestic requirements as the economy recovers. For synthetic fibers, capacity utilization remains near or over ninety percent, indicating the presence of widespread manufacturing bottlenecks. Compounding the production problem, the low level of quality in some areas of Mexican petrochemical production requires importation of goods produced domestically. For example, low tensile strength in polyester fiber has limited the growth of domestically produced fiber (Salinas, 1992).

Annual per capita consumption of textiles in Mexico is approximately 5.5 kilograms, roughly one-fourth the United States per capita consumption of approximately 20.2 kilograms.   Domestic production fills about eighty percent of all textile needs (Herrera, 1995). In addition, there is little competition in Mexican retailing. Leaders include Palacio de Hierro, Liverpool, Suburbia, Comercial Mexicana, and Fabricas de Francia. Over 50 percent of clothing is sold in small stores clustered in large cities, or by an extensive street vending system. Retailers generally lack inventory control and an organized supply system, and as such consumers are often forced to conduct extensive searches for clothing of the desired style and size (Botella et al, 1991).

Cline calculates an import elasticity of demand with respect to price of -1.3 for textiles and -1.6 for apparel, respectively (Cline, 1990). This indicates that imports of textiles and apparel into the United States will fall rapidly for those nations unable to provide competitive prices or having an overvalued currency. Indeed, many of the cyclic shifts can be traced to changes in the exchange rate. Between 1980 and 1985, the dollar appreciated twenty-two percent versus the peso, making the

Mexican apparel industry substantially more competitive than the US apparel industry. However, a ninety percent rise in the dollar relative to the currency of China resulted in an even greater competitive advantage in the market for price-sensitive substitutes. Note that the growth rate turned negative during the period of the strong peso from 1991 to 1994, indicating a lack of competitiveness by the Mexican textile industry when the advantage of low wages was removed. See TABLE 11.2.

A variety of improved international communication methods, modern production and transportation methods, and stable production technologies have increased the viability of export for high value to weight goods, such as textiles, making this sector a key toward achieving the goal of an export driven economy (Wilson, 1992). Labor costs in Mexico, at less than the equivalent of one dollar per hour, are approximately one-tenth the level of the US textile industry, providing a large competitive advantage (Botella et al, 1991). This advantage is partly countered by the high value-to-weight ratio of apparel, making imports from other nations more competitive, especially during times when the peso is overvalued. The textile industry represents about nine percent of world trade in manufactures and approximately five percent of world merchandise trade.

TABLE 11.2

CHANGE IN GROSS DOMESTIC PRODUCT,
TEXTILES AND APPAREL

Year	Percent Change
1981	5.7
1982	-4.8
1983	-5.5
1984	0.9
1985	2.6
1986	-5.2
1987	-5.1
1988	1.5
1989	3.3
1990	2.8
1991	-3.7
1992	-3.6
1993	-4.9
1994	-1.4

Source: INEGI

More than three-fourths of Mexico's textile exports go to the United States, and in many years the United States has supplied more than seventy-five percent of Mexico's textile imports. In recent years, South Korea has surpassed the United States and now holds over one-third of the Mexican textile market. US textile exports to Mexico were projected to be valued at $1.8 billion in 1996, and are expected to grow by ten to fifteen percent per year (Herrera, 1995). More than ninety-eight percent of all Mexican clothing exports go to the United States, representing approximately three percent of total imports of clothing in the United States. Clothing exports account for over 1.5 times the value of all other Mexican textile exports combined (Botella et al, 1991). As such, the Mexican textile industry must retain a large share of the total input market for Mexican apparel to remain viable.

Most restricted US imports of apparel that have been assembled abroad originate in Latin American countries.[2] Curiously, most unrestricted US imports of apparel are from Southeast Asia. This is likely because Latin American producers, reflecting a long history of import substitution and production for small markets, typically bear the burden of high cost cloth inputs (Grunwald and Flamm, 1985). As a result, many Mexican apparel firms have also moved toward sourcing from southeast Asia, decreasing the prospects for Mexican textile producers. The Mexican firms have responded by asking for increased tariff protection from producers outside of the NAFTA agreement (Mexico Business Monthly, 1998; Sutter, 1997). Moreover, Mexican firms are remarkably less productive than other foreign competitors. For example, Germany annually exports thirty times as many articles of clothing than does Mexico (Salinas, 1992). Mexico must increase productivity in the textile and apparel industry if it hopes to divert trade away from other countries and to continue to compete in the US and third country textile and apparel markets.

It is useful for comparative purposes to briefly examine the structure of the US textile industry in comparison to the Mexican producers, since most Mexican exports will need to compete in the US market. The US textile industry has two distinct components, the textile mill sector and the apparel production sector. The textile mill sector is competitive on the world-class, with large equipment and technology investments. The apparel industry, on the other hand, is rapidly shrinking in size, investment, and employment. Although imports account for less than ten percent of US textile consumption, they account for more than thirty percent of apparel consumption (Lande, 1991).

The production of apparel is shifting from developed to developing countries, such as Mexico, because of the relatively lower wages. The textile industry faces more difficult circumstances, as it does not enjoy the same pricing flexibility as does the apparel industry, which relies on highly differentiated products to create a relatively inelastic price demand (Shapiro, 1996). Nonetheless, imports of apparel by the United States have risen rapidly in relation to domestic production, from approximately thirty percent of total apparel consumption in 1962 to over ninety percent by 1983. US textiles, on the other hand, remain much more globally competitive as a result of increased technology and capital requirements (Cline, 1990).

US mills rely almost exclusively on domestic raw materials, including cotton and synthetic fibers, with US cotton prices relatively equivalent to world cotton prices. Investment in mills has been relatively high and stable in recent years. Productivity has been increasing at 3.9 percent per year, mostly as a result of investments in weaving mills. Capacity utilization approaches eighty percent. Although the degree of concentration in the industry is relatively low, the level of vertical integration with apparel producers is rising through mergers and acquisitions (Lande, 1991). Although Mexico is following the same trend, its overall level of vertical integration between the textile and apparel manufacturers is less.

US imports account for a low percentage of production of textile products. For cotton products, 29 percent of consumption results from imports. For synthetics, only 8 percent of consumption is imported. Less than four percent of US textile production is exported. However, exports to Mexico are likely to increase as Mexico shuts the door to third country textile supplies through its increased tariff, which affects third countries but not the United States or Canada. Mexican textile tariffs are rising 35 percent, up from the present 10 to 25 percent rates. This change will aid the growth of US textile exports to Mexico, which had already risen by 26 percent in 1996 (Textile World, 1997; Sutter, 1997). In some cases, the NAFTA has led to the disappearance of apparel manufacturing in the United States, while at the same time encouraging greater investment in textile manufacturing capacity, both for domestic consumption and for export (Bruner, 1998).

The majority of US apparel requirements are met with imports, either from foreign producers or from US-owned production overseas. The Far East producers have high market shares, at times approaching 50 percent of all US apparel imports. In contrast, apparel imports into the US market are growing at about 17 percent per year (Lande, 1991). In their highly influential study, Hufbauer and Schott predicted that Mexican textile and apparel exports to the United States would surge following the NAFTA. However, given the large size of the US market, there has not been a decided shift in US production away from its present path. The United States may face a trade deficit of between $1 billion and $2 billion in textiles and apparel by the end of the decade (Weintraub, 1992).

The NAFTA agreement, and subsequent changes in the technological and trade environment in North America, have had a dramatic positive impact on the textile and apparel industry. Mexican producers, in particular, have found that the new access to financial capital and improved technology have opened the door to rapidly increased exports. The Mexican textile sector, which had appeared to be losing international competitiveness, now appears ready to further increase its share of North American markets, diverting trade away from Asian producers. Likewise, the NAFTA appears to benefit US textile producers, although it has not solved the problems confronting the US apparel producers. Overall, the NAFTA appears to have strengthened the competitive position and technological capability of the North American textile and apparel industry as compared to third country producers.

---

[1] This chapter is based in part on Thomas J. Botzman, Technology and Competitiveness: A Comparison of the Mexican and US Textile and Apparel Industries, *American Society for Competitiveness*, Annual Research Volume, 1998.

[2] Certain apparel imports continue to be restricted under Section 807 of the US trade laws.

Chapter 12

Case Study: The Mexican Petrochemical and Plastics Industry

The Mexican petrochemical industry provided 3.7 percent of national GDP and about 16.3 percent of manufacturing GDP in 1993.[1] About 1.2 percent of all workers are employed by the petrochemical industry, or about 11.8 percent of manufacturing employees (INEGI, 1995). The industry takes on an added importance through its role as a symbol of national sovereignty through the political focus on the parastatal oil giant Petroleos Mexicanos, or Pemex. Even though the petrochemical sector has diminished in its leadership role in the Mexican economy, it is quite likely to continue to dominate the political dialogue on industrial policy and the role of the state for some time to come. The growth rate of the chemical and plastics sector in Mexico from 1981 to 1994 is summarized in TABLE 12.1.

The global petrochemical industry revolves around the production of three basic chemicals: ethylene, propylene, and benzene. The nature of the industry strengthens the drive for both horizontal and vertical integration, often ending further downstream at the commodity and specialty plastics sector. Consequently, the majority of important innovations in the commodity plastics industry have been made by the industry giants through the introduction of new products. However, introduction of specialty plastics has often come from the small and medium business sector. For both commodity and specialty plastics, process innovation typically follows the product innovation cycle as an incremental process.

TABLE 12.1

CHANGE IN GROSS DOMESTIC PRODUCT,
CHEMICALS AND PLASTICS

Year	Percent Change
1981	9.6
1982	2.5
1983	-1.6
1984	6.9
1985	5.8
1986	-3.5
1987	5.5
1988	2.2
1989	9.3
1990	5.2
1991	3.0
1992	2.1
1993	-2.4
1994	5.1

Source: INEGI

The Mexican petrochemical industry, as a national symbol, has experienced high visibility that has been accompanied by increasing employment in the face of slowly growing production. Further, price erosion for oil and petrochemical products has continued to pressure the sector to become more competitive with foreign producers from around the globe. Petroleos Mexicanos, or Pemex, continues to control the basic petrochemical sector, accompanied by a gradual increase in the level of independent producers of secondary petrochemicals. The sector is unique in that it has to a degree prospered in spite of recession in the domestic market. Oddly, Pemex may have been temporarily helped by the 1994 peso devaluation. Export sales are largely denominated in dollars, which provides funds for purchase of foreign exploration and production equipment.

As a result of the common border, the Mexican petrochemical industry competes directly with many U.S. firms, both in Mexico and the United States. The Mexican petrochemicals and polymer industry has an advantage over U.S. industry in raw materials feedstocks and in labor costs (Shapiro, 1996). However, the current level of production technology in Mexico is not sufficient to exploit these advantages, in the face of severely inadequate capital structure in an industry which is obviously driven by capital equipment capability. As Mexico gains the capital structure, it will first move to satisfy the high demand for consumer products. Mexico is likely to become a significant source of the commodity plastics, beginning with production for domestic consumption. Eventually, production will reach levels providing for the service of export markets, following the diffusion of technology as the international trade cycle progresses (Botzman, 1996).

The production of downstream plastic materials presents another sharp contrast between Mexico and the United States. The United States has a high level of production in the basic plastics, far outstripping the modest production in Mexico twenty times over (Anderson, 1993). Most notable among the commodity plastics is the lack of polypropylene production capacity in Mexico. Indeed, until 1991 Mexico was not producing any polypropylene, although capacity is now listed at 250,000 metric tons per year (ANIQ, 1995). Informally, it is commonly accepted in Mexico that the polypropylene plants are not able to produce at a rate anywhere near the rated capacity, as is evidenced by the industry's listing of polypropylene production for 1990 as zero. Polypropylene production in 1994 accounted for approximately twelve percent of thermoplastic resin production in Mexico, following high density polyethylene, low density polyethylene, and polyvinyl chloride in order of production volume. Much of the polypropylene shortfall can be traced to a low output of propylene monomer by Pemex. Mexico often exports crude oil, then imports monomers and specialty chemicals, and finally exports polymers. In the process, much of the cost advantage of the energy resources in Mexico is lost (Bucay, 1991). As a result, approximately two-thirds of all Mexican chemical firms report strong competition from imported products, and roughly one-half expect that the competitive pressure will increase following NAFTA (STPS and INEGI, 1995).

Production efforts for the traditional plastic materials are increasing, as technology and investment from industrialized countries find the way to Mexico, largely through strategic technology and marketing alliances. Several multinational producers, such as Hoechst-Celanese, have been in the Mexican market for several years. More recent efforts include a joint venture between Grupo Industrial Alfa and Himont to build a 150 thousand ton per year polypropylene plant, and a recent Pemex polypropylene plant based on Union Carbide technology with a rated capacity of 220 million pounds. These plants are now entering production and promise to substantially upgrade Mexican production capacity. The prominence of joint ventures and foreign investment in the industry indicates a continued need for capital and technology in Mexico. For the foreign companies, reactor and catalyst technology that has already been developed can be exported for additional profit. In addition, the U.S. multinationals can shift production between the United States and Mexico to suit future market conditions, shifts in the exchange rate, and availability of raw materials.

Consumer products made from plastics are also in short supply, as Mexico struggles to produce quantities sufficient to meet increasing domestic demand. The Mexican population, growing at 2.6 percent per year, is easily able to consume large amounts of commodity plastics. Consumption per capita has risen six fold over the past twenty-five years to fifteen kilograms, a level about one-sixth that of the United States (Banamex, 1993). Packaging makes up a large percentage of the increase in overall demand for plastics. Over 90 percent of all packaging in Mexico is made from either polyethylene or polypropylene, most of which comes from Pemex or Indelpro, a joint venture of Grupo Alfa and Himont. About 70 percent is used as film, with the remaining 30 percent used for bags. In recent years, the demand for packaging has grown about 10 percent per year, doubling the amount of imports needed to supply the shortfall in domestic polyolefin production (Ford, 1995).

Mexican exports, in the short term, will continue to follow traditional Heckscher-Ohlin international trade theory, which states that a country exports the commodity in which it has a comparative advantage, that is, the commodity in which it has a relatively abundant and cheap factor of production. The same country imports the commodity that requires a relatively scarce and expensive factor of production (Ohlin, 1933). Currently, Mexican exports are dominated by crude oil and limited amounts of natural gas. In the future, the growing exports of Heckscher-Ohlin goods will also include common plastics. This step will provide the vertical integration linkage necessary to include the petrochemical sector in the development of the Mexican economy.

The petrochemical industry in Mexico is surprisingly small for a country with a large population and relatively abundant sources of raw materials. The undersized industry requires imports to make up production deficits. Between 1980 and 1988, approximately $5.5 billion in basic petrochemicals were imported to make up for capacity deficits. The same pattern continues today, with the United States and Japan as the leading suppliers of plastic resin to the Mexican market (Ganado,

1995). At the same time, the domestic producers continue to suffer substantial losses. For example, the petrochemicals sector of Pemex lost $232.9 million in 1993 (Quintanilla and Bauer, 1996). The losses are not surprising, as sales per worker for Pemex are typically less than $20 thousand per year, about eight times less than the production for they typical U.S. worker (Banamex, 1993).

Production shortages result from the inefficient use of natural gas obtained during the oil drilling process. Capacity constraints for some of the basic petrochemicals, particularly monomers, limit production of downstream products. As a result, the potentially large petrochemical industry is unable to grow rapidly enough to meet domestic or export demand. In fact, the sector is falling farther behind in its ability to meet demand. Growth in the Mexican petrochemical industry averaged twenty-seven percent per year between 1960 and 1980, but has since slowed to less than ten percent per year (Weintraub, 1990).

The exact size of the sector is difficult to determine, as the size of the petrochemical industry changes with the various definitions of "petrochemical" by different sources. In particular, many references exclude all or part of the considerable production of Pemex, which is by far the largest producer of basic petrochemicals and also is the dominant consumer of both basic and secondary petrochemicals. It is estimated that total petrochemical industry production in Mexico represents less than one half of one percent of Mexican GNP (Weintraub, 1992), although the Mexican government suggests that the petrochemical sector comprises roughly four percent of GNP and roughly sixteen percent of manufacturing GNP (INEGI, 1994).

In contrast, the U.S. International Trade Commission provides production values on a "dry-weight" basis, that is, materials such as fillers, plasticizers, and other additives are included in the production volume. Use of USITC measurement techniques dramatically increase the reported size of the petrochemical industry. Some sources even assert that the Mexican petrochemical and plastics industry is larger than the Mexican automobile industry (Bucay, 1991). In reality, the petrochemical industry probably represents between one half of one percent and five percent of Mexican GNP, changing rapidly with increases and decreases of production by Pemex versus other industrial sectors. In any case, the petrochemical and plastics sector represents a large slice of Mexico's productive capacity and ability to compete in industries downstream from its petroleum resource endowment. Capacity, production, and value of the basic and secondary chemical sectors in 1993 are summarized in TABLE 12.2.

TABLE 12.2

MEXICAN PETROCHEMICAL CAPACITY,
PRODUCTION, AND VALUE, 1993

	Total	Basic	Secondary	Other
Capacity (million tons)	19,838	4,632	6,392	9,085
Production (million tons)	17,638	5,074	4,935	7,629
Value (million new pesos)	6,200	622	3,792	1,786

Source: INEGI

It is, moreover, very difficult to determine the actual size of plastics industry segments in Mexico, particularly as a result of the large "underground" economy. There are roughly 3,000 registered plastic processors in Mexico, with approximately the same number unregistered. Approximately two thousand firms are classified as part of the petrochemical industry by the Mexican government (STPS and INEGI, 1995). Employment totals about 125 thousand workers, with most firms producing films and bags, industrial parts, reinforced parts, and plastic products for home use (INEGI, 1995). See Table 12.3.

TABLE 12.3

PERSONNEL EMPLOYED IN THE
MEXICAN PLASTICS INDUSTRY,
PERCENT BY SECTOR, 1994

Product	Percent
Molded shapes and pieces	16.5
Polyethylene bags and films	16.2
Packaging and polystyrene pieces	14.4
Games	10.8
Articles for the home	10.3
Others	31.8

Source: Author's calculations based on 1994 INEGI data

Studies of the industry are further complicated by the dual public and private faces of the industry. The dominance of Pemex in many sectors of the industry prevents obtaining a clear reading of important aspects of the industry, such as productivity and costs by product line. As such, most of the discussion of the impact of free trade has been concentrated on the first stages of oil and petrochemical production. However, an increasing amount of data is available for the plastics industry, providing a much clearer picture of the structure of downstream production and distribution. The data also provides an opportunity to assess the growing need for foreign technology.

Some observers estimate that the Mexican petrochemicals sector requires up to $10 billion of plant investment simply to meet domestic demand (Quintanilla and Bauer, 1996). Mexico is beginning to address the need for increased investment in plant and equipment, totaling over one billion dollars in 1991 and 1992 alone. However, estimates are that the present rate of investment must more than double over the next five years just to keep pace with the rapid increase in domestic demand, with some estimates indicating a need for $10 billion just to meet domestic demand (Quintanilla and Bauer, 1996). At present only about five percent of firms in the sector report have a new production process, while nearly one-half of firms in the sector report having mature technology (STPS and INEGI, 1995). Clearly, increased investment is required just to remain competitive in the domestic market, let alone support exports. Unfortunately, investment fell to $608 million by 1994, and it is unlikely that Mexico will have the resources in the near term to modernize the petrochemical and polymer sector (ANIQ, 1995). As a step toward financial transparency, Pemex has recently published balance sheets for each of the operating companies, providing a much needed opportunity for potential investors to estimate returns on potential equity investments (Quintanilla and Bauer, 1996). The ability to attract portfolio equity and direct foreign investment may reduce the need for increased loans, permitting a market driven expansion of production capacity. It may also reduce the tendency to create extra jobs at Pemex as a reward for political support.

Further, investment in research and development remains low at only 0.6 percent of industry income, a level similar to that of most Mexican manufacturers but far below the levels typically encountered in the United States and other developed economies. More than one-half of all Mexican petrochemical producers report that they do not conduct any research and development activity in-house, relying completely on purchases for transfer of technology, with most of the capital equipment purchased from firms in the United States or China (Ganado, 1995).

Less than three percent of industry income is used for the purchase or transfer of technology, again retarding the adoption of modern petrochemical production techniques (STPS and INEGI, 1995).

Low cost raw materials, when coupled with additional capital, will provide Mexico with the comparative advantage for production and export of basic plastics. Mexico will become "process" oriented in the petrochemical field, relying on conventional catalyst systems for production of plastics. The United States will continue on its recent trend toward more "product" innovation and consumption (Teece, 1991). After all, as the product innovation leader for the chemical industry, the United States supplies over 14 thousand commercial chemical products (Quijada, 1991). Before Mexico can gain a "product" orientation, Pemex will need to rationalize its product line, permitting greater competition and vertical integration in other areas (Bucay, 1991).

According to the product life cycle model, new products require highly skilled labor for development and production. However, as a product matures, it becomes standardized. The process technology licensed by Mexico will over time become standardized technology. More than one-half of the sector's firms report purchases of domestic technology, and nearly one out of each six firms reports purchases of technology from the United States (STPS and INEGI, 1995). Eventually, mass production will be accomplished using less skilled labor, and with a lower unit labor cost (Vernon, 1966). As such, the competitive advantage eventually shifts from the developed country, the United States, to the less developed country, Mexico.

In the case of highly engineered polymers, production may eventually shift from the United States to Mexico, although with a necessary time lag of several decades as Mexico assimilates process technology. The abundant supply of raw materials and lower cost labor dictates the eventual shift. However, such a shift requires that Mexico first progress through a stage of production that satisfies demand for the basic plastics, a process that may take several decades. During this stage, the production infrastructure, both capital and labor, will be prepared for the shift to emerging technologies. In particular, Mexico will begin to realize the benefits of vertical integration: economies of scale, increased value added, and reduced transportation costs (Quijada, 1991). The value added will grow rapidly as Mexico captures not only the value of plastics production and processing, but also the value of the production of monomers from crude oil and natural gas.

In the long term, technology developments will have an impact on the types of products produced and consumed in both countries. The United States is already shifting to increased consumption of specialty polymers. Mexico must first proceed toward satisfaction of basic demand before moving toward specialty polymers. Gruber, Mehta and Vernon indicate that research and development provide this "dynamic" comparative advantage, as contrasted with the "static" comparative advantage presented by the Heckscher-Ohlin model (Gruber et al, 1967). The "dynamic" nature of technology changes creates trade different from that resulting from the traditional input factors of labor and capital. As international investment revitalizes the Mexican petrochemical industry, technology will initially flow through increasingly rapid licensing of process technology (Quijada, 1991).

The importance of technology transfer for development of the Mexican petrochemical sector highlights the dynamic factors involved in U.S.-Mexico trade. The traditional static model, in effect, is unable to explain the future direction of petrochemical sector trade. Arndt states, "It is widely believed that regional trade liberalization will give rise to a northward flow of certain agricultural products and of Heckscher-Ohlin goods (standardized products made with standard labor and capital), while southward flows will be dominated by product-cycle goods (made with human capital, R&D, specialized labor, etc.)." Using the framework presented by Arndt, the United States will become increasing focused on "product" development of plastics (Arndt, 1991).

---

[1] This chapter is based in part on Thomas J. Botzman, Technology and Trade in the Mexican Thermoplastic Industry, *The Anahuac Journal*, Universidad Anahuac del Sur, Spring/Summer 1997.

Chapter 13

Case Study: The Mexican Steel Industry

Until the 1980s, the production of steel in Mexico was roughly split between parastatal production and private production.[1] With the privatization of the steel industry now complete, Mexican steel is enjoying a new level of competitiveness in the world market. As recently as 1991 parastatal production contributed 4,114 thousand tons, or approximately fifty-two percent of production. Following the privatization of Sidermex, the dominant share of steel production and distribution now belongs to the private firms, including many more small minimill operations.

The industry employs nearly two percent of all manufacturing personnel, and creates 0.2 percent of employment nationally. Employment has fallen from 67 thousand workers in 1989 to 41 thousand by 1993, largely as a result of the privatization of the parastatal firms (INEGI, 1995). The downturn in employment has not reflected a decay in the strength of the industry, rather it has indicated a new competitiveness for the industry. Mexican steel production has risen on average seventeen percent per year during the 1990s, rising from seven percent of North American production to over nine percent (Martinez, 1995). It is quite likely that Mexico will soon produce more steel than Canada. The growth rate of the basic metals sector in Mexico from 1981 to 1994 is summarized in TABLE 13.1.

TABLE 13.1

CHANGE IN GROSS DOMESTIC PRODUCT
BASIC METALS

Year	Percent Change
1981	4.9
1982	-9.3
1983	-6.2
1984	11.6
1985	1.0
1986	-6.9
1987	11.1
1988	5.4
1989	2.6
1990	8.0
1991	-3.5
1992	-0.1
1993	5.1
1994	8.6

Source: INEGI

As the steel industry in Mexico was privatized and the NAFTA was signed, the firms began to view trade and technology from a distinctly North American perspective. This is reflected by the three Mexican firms that have joined the American Iron and Steel Institute since 1993: Altos Hornos de Mexico, Hylsamex, and Ispat Mexicana (Schmidt, 1995). Further, the Multilateral Steel Agreement, long in the works, is again being held up over disputes over the European Union's subsidies to steelmakers. The net result is that the North American steel industry has taken an increasingly regional focus. The three NAFTA partner nations appear to be more interested in maintaining a separate North American market than in encouraging greater multilateral cooperation (Fenton, 1995).

The global steel industry, which has been rapidly restructuring during the past three decades, will face significant changes under trade liberalization. These changes will include both shifts in production locations on an international scale and further expansion of the role of the new technology minimill producers, newer steel producing facilities using high scrap inputs and electric furnaces, into the traditional markets of the larger integrated mills (see Botzman, 1991; Williams and Botzman, 1994; Crandall 1981, 1987, 1993).

The Mexican steel industry is likely to face many of the same opportunities and challenges as are facing the global steel industry. The global steel industry, after experiencing stagnant growth in demand for nearly three decades, is beginning to grow again. Current world consumption is estimated at 611 million metric tons, but is expected to grow to 720 million tons by the year 2000, according to the International Iron and Steel Institute. Most of this increase will result from increased demand and production from China (Samways, 1994). The developing countries now consume 15 percent of world steel production, up from 9 percent in 1973. Third World steel consumption grew by over 8 percent per year from 1960 until 1979, but slowed to 1.4 percent per year from 1979 until 1987, largely as a result of slow to negative economic growth in Latin America. In a recent study, Tilton concluded that the intensity of steel use in developing countries has risen by approximately 14.4 percent per year. This growth was sufficient to counteract reduced growth in demand resulting from slower growth in GDP, which stagnated during the eighties (Tilton, 1990). If economic growth accelerates in Mexico, it can be concluded that the growth in steel demand will intensify and accelerate considerably, perhaps reaching growth rates of nearly 20 percent per year in the near future.

The traditional steel industry was dominated by large integrated mills that produced a variety of steel mill products. Recently, minimills have specialized in the production of smaller quantities of steel with a narrow product line. In doing so, the minimills have created a more flexible and price responsive steel industry. The price responsive minimills provide a striking contrast to the inflexibility of the integrated mill producers, which have traditionally followed an oligopolistic pricing model. As such, the dynamics of choosing a steel supplier based on quality, lead time, and price has been altered. By changing the traditional structure of steel supply, the capacity considerations for a steel supplier have been reduced to somewhat smaller levels that favor the minimill producers (Erceg, 1989).

The minimills have two technologies that have separated them from the integrated mills. First, the minimills primarily use electric furnaces for heating steel. Although this technology was first implemented by Heroult in 1900, its rapid introduction has occurred over the past 30 years. Use of the electric furnace removes almost all of the usual preliminary steps in the steel production process, relying instead upon the use of scrap steel. Second, nearly all steel production is linked to continuous caster technology. Although continuous casters have been added to integrated mills, this can be costly and difficult as compared to implementation in greenfield operations. Further, the continuous caster is better suited to use of smaller billets as produced in the minimills (Scherrer, 1988). Noting that the mean age of minimills is about 6 years, compared with 22 years for the integrated mills, we can assume that the minimills typically have substantially newer technology embodied in the mill operations. This in turn leads to an enhanced ability of the minimill producers to respond to price changes facing the industry (Acs, 1988).

The pattern for Mexican production is likely to mirror that of the United States and Canada, where the minimills have almost pushed the integrated mills out of the markets for wire rods, wire and wire products, structural shapes, and bars. Further, the minimill markets have generally been able to fight imported steel better than have the traditional integrated mill products (Acs, 1988). As the minimills enter the market for hot and cold rolled steel they will begin to dominate nearly all industry segments. Consequently, the majority of steel production in the next century will be controlled by the minimill producers, such as Nucor. Nucor has shown the highest sales and earnings growth rates of U.S. steel firms over the past 25 years. Much of the increase in sales has been in steel shapes and sheet steel, areas traditionally dominated by the integrated producers. Nucor's success relies heavily on new technology, such as electromagnetic braking in the steel bath to remove surface imperfections and a method to vary the thickness of cast slab (Anderson, 1995).

The restructuring of the global steel supply has been accompanied by the rapid increase in the number of international joint ventures. In 1960, U.S. and Canadian production was dominated by firms that were vertically integrated and linked through interest groups, such as the Cleveland Group and the Cleveland Cliffs Company (Scheuerman, 1990). Vertical integration was a natural outgrowth of both the reduction in raw material and finished product shipping costs and the prevailing strategies of the steel producers (Burnham, 1993). The vertically integrated interest groups controlled over one-half of all U.S. and Canadian steel production and provided an effective shield against competition, particularly from foreign firms. In recent years, these interest groups have faded in power and have been replaced by international joint ventures or international ownership. Over 25 percent of all U.S. production is now owned by foreign interests. Further, the sharing of technology has become widespread in the industry, creating a new worldwide web of linkages (Scheuerman, 1990). The increased foreign direct investment in new capital technology is likely to continue to alter trade patterns in the future. This sharing of technology has been cited as a reason for the rapid increase in labor productivity in the U.S. steel industry during recent years. Labor productivity in the U.S. steel industry rose by 4.3 percent per year from 1985 to 1990, compared to less than one percent for the overall business sector (Burnham, 1993).

In the case of Mexico, the expected growth of the economy will increase the need for steel throughout all of the traditional downstream sectors. In particular, construction and automotive markets will grow rapidly. Several large projects, such as the construction of a highway linking Guadalajara and Mexico City and new railroads and ports, will require very large quantities of steel (Lazaroff, 1993). The NAFTA effectively provides additional access to the financial capital required for the expansion of Mexican steel capacity, as is evidenced by the growing number of joint ventures between Mexican steel producers and multinationals from the United States and Canada. Government and business cooperation is also occurring across borders. Hylsa and the U.S. Department of Energy are cooperating in a joint venture on a new technology for recycling of waste oxides, direct steelmaking. A demonstration project will be located at a Stelco facility on Lake Erie (Schmidt, 1995).

Mexican producers are generally assumed to be lower quality producers than those in the United States and Canada, limiting opportunities for exports to the United States. However, some smaller Mexican steel producers are already installing specialized capacity to serve niche markets, both domestically and internationally. For example, Teknik S.A. de C.V. of Monterrey has installed new furnaces and an automated molding system to serve the specialty castings market. Clients include subsidiaries of several multinational firms, including General Electric, Nissan, General Motors, John Deere, and Caterpillar (Foundry, 1993).

Mexico exports approximately 500 thousand tons of steel to the United States each year, holding about three percent of the U.S. import market. Steel imports to the United States from Mexico generally arrive by truck, rather than following the traditional low-cost water transportation favored by the global steel industry. Primary sites of entry for steel imports to Mexico include Matamoros with 31.1 percent of imports, Tuxpan with 19.3 percent, Veracruz with 16.0 percent, and Puerta Negras with 12.8 percent (AHMSA, 1993). A consequence of the ground transport link between the Mexican and U.S. markets is that Mexico must look to the U.S. market for sale of excess steel production. Following the peso devaluation of December 1994, the Mexican steel producers responded to the nearly fifty percent drop in domestic demand for steel with an increase of fifty percent in exports. AHMSA, for example, won contracts for 400 thousand tons of steel in only 18 days following the devaluation of the peso (Zelade, 1996).

Although electricity, gas, and scrap input prices have risen, the increases have not offset the advantage of the devalued peso, providing a considerable export advantage (Cabrera, 1995).

The Mexican steel industry has dramatically increased spending on technology development and implementation since 1991, with total spending approaching 2.5 billion dollars (Zelade, 1996). Mexican companies are increasingly conscious that "medium quality steel" will not find an export market, and that technology must be at the same level as the international production leaders (Fonseca, 1995). Spending to upgrade and improve capacity at integrated mills is continuing and expanding following the privatization of the steel industry and the opening of markets. For example, APM of Monterrey is modernizing its hot strip and plate mill. Hylsa is installing a $300 million, 900 thousand tons per year thin slab casting/rolling mill complex in Monterrey. This upgrade will be the first to use Nippon direct current shaft furnace technology, indicating an increased willingness for Mexican steel to import technology and equipment. High production rates of up to 200 tons per hour will result from charges that include up to 45 percent scrap input, increasing the productive outlet for recycled steel in Mexico (Samways, 1994). Hylsa's new flat steel plant is only the eighth in the world and the first in Latin American employing the new Compact Steel Production technology. This results in substantial cost savings because sponge iron prices are lower than scrap prices (Cabrera, 1995). Joint ventures will be used to market the steel from the new mill, with cooperative efforts through Sumitomo of Japan, Usinor Sacilor of France, and Thyssen AG of Germany (Huskonen, 1995). Hylsa has plans for a 480 thousand tons per year greenfield operation near Monterrey to produce rolled steel. The technology is based on several cooperative efforts between Hylsa and Nucor, the most successful of the U.S. minimill producers. The plant is projected to increase Hylsa's rolled steel production by thirty percent while drastically cutting labor and energy costs (Lazaroff, 1993).

It has been estimated that more than half of Mexico's steel production technology employs direct reduced iron (Whipp, 1997). Hylsa introduced direct reduced-iron into their mills in 1957, saving on scrap prices and reducing the space needed for blast furnaces. Hylsa invests $8 million per year on research and development of direct reduced-iron technology, making it the second largest firm in the world in the field. Hylsa produces 7 million metric tons per year of direct reduced-iron using Mexican technology, and an addition 17.8 million tons using U.S. technology. The Mexican process is currently in use in Brazil, Venezuela, Indonesia, Iraq, Iran, India, and Malaysia (Cabrera, 1995). New scheduled capacity for production of direct reduced-iron is planned by Hylsa, 750,000 tons per year; Ispat America, 1.5 million tons per year; and Ispat Mexicana, 1.2 million tons per year. Trade in direct reduced-iron is expected to grow from 7.7 million metric tons in 1995 to 19.55 million metric tons by 2005 (Isenberg-O'Loughlin, 1995).

Several minimill producers are also upgrading operations and installing capacity in Mexico. The efforts are spread geographically across the country, serving local markets and reducing transportation costs. Recent capacity upgrades include those by Aceros DM in San Luis Potosi, Compania Siderurgica de California in Mexicali, Deacero in Monterrey, F.ES.ZA. in Zacatecas, Talleres y Aceros in Orizaba, and Siderurgica Tultitlan in Mexico City (Samways, 1994). Mexico has an enormous opportunity to capitalize on minimill technology through increasing the rate of recycling of steel scrap. Out of 13.2 million tons of domestic steel production, only 2.2 million tons originate from scrap. Of this amount, only 190 metric tons come from post-consumer scrap, leading to a quarterly scrap shortage of over 110 thousand metric tons (Cabrera, 1995).

It has been argued that the export of technology from the United States to other countries typically follows a model of using the same mass-production methods abroad, often leading to failure in the host country. The inappropriate transfer of technology then actually retards development of the domestic industry. However, the Mexican steel industry is an example of where the new minimill technology has been used to produce at a low cost in a relatively unstable international environment. This contrasts with the relatively slow adoption of minimill technology by the integrated steel plants in the United States (Acs, 1988). In the United States and Canada, the introduction of minimill technology has led to the regional production of steel away from the domination of the Great Lakes producers. This change in production location will be very important and visible in Mexico's future. The minimill will be strongly favored in Mexico as a result of the relatively low capital investment required, the possibility of locating near the regional market to lower transportation costs, and the specialization in bars and structural steel as needed for the rapidly industrializing economy (Scherrer, 1988). Mexican production, as driven by minimill facilities, will likely be dispersed more evenly across the country than is U.S. or Canadian production.

---

[1] This chapter is based in part on Thomas J. Botzman, Prospects for the North American Steel Industry, *Ciencia Ergo Sum*, Universidad Autonoma del Estado de Mexico, 1997.

Chapter 14

Case Study: The Mexican Automobile Industry

The Mexican automobile industry plays a key role in the development of a modern manufacturing sector. In 1994, automobile production comprised 2.7 percent of national GNP, and 12.1 percent of manufacturing GNP. The auto sector created 0.7 percent of the jobs nationally, and over 7.3 percent of the jobs in the manufacturing sector (INEGI, 1995). With sales of over 86 million pesos in 1991, the automobile industry is by far the single largest manufacturing sector in Mexico. It is estimated that 70 thousand workers are employed in auto production, 145 thousand in auto parts production, 120 thousand in auto parts maquiladoras, and 80 thousand in auto distribution (Maldonado, 1995). Mexico controls 13 percent of North American parts production, and nearly 6 percent of final assembly operations (Blum, 1998).

The automobile sector has three key parts, production of automobiles, production of motors and parts, and tires and rubber products. The production of automobiles is the largest of the three, with fifty-seven percent of the value of the sector (INEGI, 1995). The growth of the auto sector is a key to providing increased employment opportunities in the future, both directly and through linkages into the auto parts, steel, glass, and plastics sectors. The automobile sector clearly has the opportunity for significant multiplier effects in creating jobs, noting that close to fifty percent of U.S. GDP is connected to the automobile industry (Maldonado, 1995).[1] The automobile parts sector, on the other hand, has not developed into an effective global competitor. The Mexican government has apparently recognized the difficulty of focusing on too many sectors for development and sought to relax trade barriers for imported goods with automotive decrees in 1983 and 1989 that removed domestic content requirements (Bannister et al, 1996). The December 1989 Automotive Decree removed the pressure to develop the national auto parts industry, perhaps as a reflection of the lag between Mexican production capabilities and that of the global parts suppliers (UNCTC, 1992). The 1989 Decree did, however, reinforce Mexico's place as a component of the regional auto industry and increased the focus on exports (Blum, 1998).

The automobile sector has emerged as a leading exporter, in contrast to the previous status as net importer. As recently as the beginning of the 1980s, the automotive industry was still internally oriented. The import of automobiles contributed nearly fifteen percent of Mexico's total trade deficit (UNCTC, 1992). The devaluation dramatically reduced the domestic consumption of automobiles and trucks in Mexico, falling from 623 thousand units in 1994 to about 189 thousand units in 1995. Exports rose from forty-eight percent of production to eighty percent of production (Ferris, 1996).

Much of Mexico's success as an exporter has been attributed to lower wage rates and the lower rate of union membership in some parts of the country (Studer, 1998). It is estimated that the wage difference provides an approximate savings of $800 per unit produced (Bannister et al, 1996). The wage cost has differential has been increasing during the past decade. For example, labor costs at the Puebla Volkswagen plant have dropped from over 10 percent of total cost in 1992 to 3 percent by 1995 (Juárez Núñez, 1998). Noting that the modern automobile industry is more labor intensive than other key industries, this advantage will be difficult to overcome without further reducing the proportion of product cost traced to labor inputs (Drucker, 1990).

As a part of the global automobile industry, Mexican producers face the challenge of the latest technological transformation facing the industry, including the introduction of lean production techniques pioneered by the Japanese producers. The Japanese system of lean production of automobiles differs from the traditional mass production methods of Ford in that in mass production one worker typically runs one machine to do the same repetitive task. In lean production, workers rotate among a number of tasks to keep machines running near capacity

(Graves, 1994). Further, changes in the areas of electronics and materials technologies will radically transform the production of automobiles. Tooling, design, and production will increasingly need to become more flexible to respond to the rapid changes in the market for automobiles. Not only will Mexico need to be continue to upgrade technological capability to export but also to serve the domestic market, particularly in response to increasing environmental concerns and bottlenecks in the production of engines and automobile parts (Unger, 1991).

Mexican automobile and automobile part production is centered in three areas. Most production is located in Mexico City and the nearby States of Mexico and Puebla; however, environmental measures continue to add pressure to locate in other areas. The northeast and midwest of the country, in the corridor from Monterrey to Guadalajara, encompass the second region surrounding much of the industrial base of Mexico. The third area is located in the northwest of the country, near the border, led by Hermosillo, Ciudad Juarez, Tijuana, Mexicali, and Chihuahua. Several new plants have been built in northern Mexico, including plants by Nissan in Aguascalientes, General Motors and Chrysler in Coahuila, and Ford in Chihuahua and Sonora (Bannister et al, 1996).

The northwest area is also the primary location for maquiladora production, hosting 120 maquiladora plants for parts in 1994 (Maldonado, 1995). General Motors controls 50 plants, employing more than 25,000 workers, trailed by Ford with over 7,000 workers (Studer, 1998). The high number of maquiladoras has led to dependence on imports of raw materials and parts throughout the industry. The automobile sector in 1991 imported nearly sixty percent of all production inputs, a level nearly twice as high as that of the textile, chemical, and metals sectors (STPS and INEGI, 1995). The auto parts maquiladoras are manufacturing engines, transmissions, and brake parts. The auto maquiladoras are small, with less than 125 workers. General Motors hopes to source $1.4 billion of automotive components from Mexico by the turn of the century (Ferris, 1996). Employment in the maquiladoras by transportation equipment firms has risen rapidly, from 4.5 percent of all workers in 1979 to 21.5 percent in 1990. Electronics and automotive firms continue to control over sixty percent of all maquiladora workers (Wilson, 1992).

Mexico has a two-tiered structure of automobile production. Modern high-technology production facilities produce for export markets, while older facilities continue to produce for the domestic market (Shaiken, 1994). The Ford - Hermosillo plant represents approximately one-fourth of the total export capacity of the Mexican automobile industry (Bannister et al, 1996). The older plants generally have shorter production runs, some producing only a few hundred units of a model per year. The different production styles are very evident even to the casual observer in Mexico where luxury automobiles, such as the Lexus or BMW, run alongside hundreds of Volkswagen Beetles manufactured in the state of Puebla.

The five largest automobile producers in Mexico are all under foreign ownership. The U.S. Big Three (General Motors, Ford, and Chrysler) are joined by Japan's Nissan and Germany's Volkswagen. The international presence has a long history, beginning with Ford in 1925 (Maldonado, 1995). Some of the production plants are new and employ world class technology, such as Ford's Hermosillo assembly plant, while others are decidedly low-tech, such as Volkswagen's Puebla assembly plant (Maartens, 1991). The high technology plants were built during the 1980s, following the Automotive Decree of 1977 that signaled the shift from emphasis on domestic production under the import-substitution policy to an emphasis on export production (López-de-Silanes, 1991). Nearly all of the production is of subcompact and compact automobiles. Production by company in 1994 is noted below.

TABLE 14.1

AUTOMOBILE PRODUCTION IN MEXICO, 1994

Producer	Units Produced
Chrysler	46,816
Ford	26,804
General Motors	41,962
Nissan	92,286
Volkswagen	144,517

Source: INEGI

Given the international competitiveness and constant change in the automobile market, it is difficult to predict the future direction of production of automobiles in Mexico. The U.S. International Trade Commission remains unsure about the impact of NAFTA on trade in automobiles. Hufbauer and Schott predict that four new features will arrive with the reduction in trade barriers: Mexican concentration on light trucks and entry-level cars, increased Mexican production of auto parts, increased health of the North American automobile market and producers, and a decline in union jobs in the United States and Canada (Weintraub, 1992).

Nonetheless, the drive to acquire new technology necessary for global competition in the automotive industry will continue to force Mexican firms to increase joint venture linkages with firms from the United States, Asia, and Europe (Maartens, 1991). In particular, firms will seek to create alliances which share extremely high engineering and design costs (Studer, 1998). Examples of present joint ventures include Ford and Grupo Alfa, through Nemak; Ford, Grupo Alfa and Grupo Visa, through Vitroflex and Carplastic; and General Motors with Grupo Condumex through Condumex Autoparts. Extending previous cooperation, Mazda engineers supplied Ford with a considerable body of technology for the Hermosillo plant, which was the first factory in the world to combine stamping, manufacturing, and assembly at one facility (Studer, 1998). The joint ventures produce for both the domestic market and the export market (López-de-Silanes, 1991). Assistance has been provided in not only product design and equipment, but also in quality control and employee training programs. The Hermosillo plant was used as an "important lab for learning new ways of doing things" (Haigh, 1992).Many of the Mexican parts suppliers also hope to increase domestic content in automobiles produced in Mexico, growing from the currently very low levels (Maldonado, 1995). Ford ensured that just-in-time inputs would be available through encouragement to supplier firms to located near the plant. Carplastic, instrument panels; CISA, seats; CIMA, carpets; PEMSA, seat belts; Aurolin, paints; Goodyear, tires; and Pittsburgh Paints, paints; all made substantial investments to locate near the new plant (Bannister et al, 1996).

As the manufacturers upgraded the capital equipment in the newer plants, they recognized the need to complement the new equipment with modern worker training and organization, combining both the "hard" and "soft" components of manufacturing technology (Garcia, 1998). The high-technology plants followed three strategies in creating a skilled work force. First, the plants selected young and highly motivated workers with no production experience. In many cases, the plants now hire workers in their teens as a means of increasing motivation and reducing turnover rates, some of which had approached 100 percent per year. Second, the plants provide a very high level of training for the workers, reflecting the belief that new equipment increases the knowledge needs of more than one-half of all workers (STPS and INEGI, 1995). Many of the new workers spend four months in classroom training before they ever see the production plant. At the General Motors Silao plant, over one-fourth of the time is dedicated to creation and support of work teams, a new concept for most of the workers (García, 1998). Finally, the plant employ experienced managers from international operations or other production plants in Mexico as supervisors in the training and production process (Shaiken, 1994). By 1995, the management of the Hermosillo plant was entirely Mexican (Bannister et al, 1996).

TABLE 14.2

MEXICAN AUTOMOTIVE AND MANUFACTURING
EMPLOYMENT, 1940 - 1993

Year	Automobile Workers	Total Manufacturing Workers	Percent of Manufacturing Workers
1940	1,328	289,908	0.46
1945	444	475,461	0.09
1950	3,701	698,611	0.53
1960	16,059	791,458	2.03
1965	34,936	1,343,510	2.60
1970	60,000	1,726,000	3.48
1975	97,000	2,002,000	4.85
1980	121,200	2,417,000	5.01
1981	135,600	2,542,000	5.33
1982	118,700	2,485,000	4.78
1983	94,300	2,310,000	4.08
1984	108,500	2,361,000	4.60
1985	132,300	2,487,000	5.32
1986	117,700	2,387,000	4.93
1987	123,300	2,305,000	5.35
1988	135,500	2,354,000	5.76
1989	170,300	2,492,720	6.83
1990	180,742	2,510,276	7.20
1991	189,511	2,498,769	7.58
1992	185,095	2,447,150	7.56
1993	170,472	2,324,976	7.33

Source: INEGI

Education and training played a strong role in the rapid success of the Hermosillo plant. Students from the state of Sonora complete on average eight years of schooling, higher than most other Mexican states. Further, over ninety percent of the plant workers have finished high school and nearly one-third have been to a university or professional school. Every new employee receives four months of training (Shaiken, 1991). Many employees received up to eighteen months of training, with much of the training program conducted in Japan, Belgium, and Spain (Haigh, 1992). The Hermosillo plant uses Mazda's total quality management program, resulting from Ford's interest formed during benchmarking visits to several Mazda facilities in Japan. Training is conducted in Hermosillo, at Mazda's Hiroshima plant, and at Ford's plants in Valencia, Spain; Ghent, Belgium; and Detroit (Bannister et al, 1996).

---

[1] It is not clear how this estimate was generated, although it is obvious that the US auto industry purchases inputs from a wide variety of suppliers. It was not specified whether this calculation includes inter-industry purchases and sales, which are not included in GDP calculations.

Chapter 15

Summary and Conclusion

The impact of technology on industrial competitiveness has been studied thoroughly by academics and industry practitioners. In the case of Mexico, many of the previous academic studies focus on the role of government in directing development and transfer of technology, providing an extensive view of the leadership established by the Mexican government during the import-substitution period (see, for example, Porrúa, 1994). However, relatively little has been written to describe the development of technological capacity at the level of Mexican industry. Recent literature and government surveys have provided a window of opportunity to not only assess the role of industry in Mexican technology development, but also to gauge possible strengths and weaknesses of the system as Mexico looks to the future. In this book, case studies of four major industrial sectors (textiles, plastics, metals, and automobiles) serve as a basis for examining the current state of industrial technology in Mexico. Approaching technology development from the viewpoint of industry appears to hold promise for a more competitive Mexico. The sectors provide a diverse range of size, firm age, capital intensity, and ownership patterns, dictating unique approaches to technology practice in each sector.

Mexican technological capacity has been described by several authors as backward, lacking the competitive level to compete in global markets. In particular, many authors point to a lack of sustainable foreign direct investment in the creation of a modern capital structure. The Mexican government, through recent changes in law and policy, has sought to create an environment which encourages foreign investment. Much of the foreign direct investment is being formed through joint ventures, foreign ownership, and alliances, replacing the Mexican model of import substitution industrialization. The newly formed influence of foreign firms is clearly increasing the amount and proportion of funds that the Mexican firms now spend for technology transfer, research and development, and training.

In the past, the Mexican government controlled virtually all technology programs, and it continues to provide seventy-eight percent of all funding for science and technology programs (OECD, 1994). The shift toward greater industrial and academic participation, although only in its infancy, follows the prescription of Porter (1990), "Government policy will fail if it remains the only source of national competitive advantage. Successful policies work in those industries where underlying determinants of competitive advantage are present and where government reinforces them." Clearly, the shift toward increased industrial participation in technology development and transfer appears to be a very positive step toward improved industrial competitiveness. In particular, cultural norms, the legal structure, and macroeconomic policy are changing to encourage increased receptivity to both in-house and external technology. Pockets of technological leadership are beginning to appear, particularly in the automobile and steel industries. Nonetheless, the current state of technological capacity by Mexican industry is not sufficient to compete on a wide scale with firms from the developed economies nor with southeast Asian firms.

Recent government efforts have been aimed at not only deregulation of technology policy, but also the decentralization of science and technology to state and local control. These efforts include, for example, the increased financial support provided to educational institutions outside of Mexico City. The costly government research laboratories of CONACYT are being slowly replaced by research at the university level. Moreover, the recent trend toward development of industry - academic linkages through the establishment of technology incubator programs around the country is a critical step in creating a sustainable technology base which serves the needs of the business community. However, in the long term, technological capacity in Mexico will continue to grow at a pace sustainable by the continued reform of the educational system. Substantially more engineers will need to be prepared for careers in private industry, and a larger group of students will need to be given the opportunity to enter and complete graduate studies. Over time, clusters of innovative Mexican firms may begin serving as a novel and effective springboard for widespread technological development.

The enhanced participation of the micro, small, and medium size businesses in Mexico is critical to the eventual success of any plan for technology development. Not only do the small firms employ nearly half of all factory workers, they also represent the continued cultural importance of the family in the business community. In addition, the smaller firms often bear a higher proportion of the new product and process development costs, especially as compared to subsidiaries of foreign MNCs which import technology from the parent. The small firms, through their ability to move rapidly, have the potential to adopt new niche technology rapidly. Further, many of the smaller firms can adopt generic technology, such as just-in-time or CAD/CAM, to increase productivity throughout the value chain. By focusing on process technology rather than product introductions the smaller firms will be prepared to provide inputs for the larger Mexican firms and multinational corporations. Further, the increased development of export markets for small firms will not only provide foreign exchange stability but also increased technology linkages with foreign firms.

Multinational corporations, in contrast, already have access to foreign technology and export markets. The majority of a Mexican subsidiary's technology is imported from abroad, substantially reducing the need to spend for domestic technology. The MNC's access to foreign technology does, however, provide opportunity to look for other technology-driven advantages. The ability to create backward linkages to small business suppliers and forward linkages into the Mexican and international markets places the MNCs in a strategic position to promote improved process and product quality. In addition, the maquiladora operations of MNCs may also play a role by importing both generic and advanced technology for the production of export products. Although the maquiladoras have not generally been effective technology transfer agents in the past, they have the potential to substantially impact the growth of technological capacity in the future. In particular, the maquiladoras will play a key role in the competitiveness of the automobile industry and, consequently, the northwest region of Mexico.

Training is essential to the updating of the skills of the Mexican worker as needed to obtain the spillover effects from use of generic technology. With an expanded focus on technological capability for firms of all sizes, the need to offer additional training will quickly come to the forefront. Currently, only about one-third of Mexican firms provide training programs (Herrera, 1993). However, the amount of training programs being offered is growing rapidly, especially in the larger firms of the chemical, steel, and automobile industries. Each of the industry segments studied reports that over seventy percent of new employees now receive training, and that the use of external trainers is rising (STPS and INEGI, 1995). In particular, the use of training will be essential to the formation of quality culture in Mexico. The shift toward increased training is an unmistakable sign that Mexican industry does intend to fully compete in many international markets.

The Mexican manufacturing sector has continued to modernize despite the uneven performance of the overall economy. The focus on export markets can only help to improve the quality of goods produced for both the domestic and export markets. The steel and automobile industries, in particular, have continued to invest heavily in capital equipment. The textile and plastics sectors, on the other hand, face increasingly difficult futures as the market continues to open to foreign competition. A considerable amount of modernization is being used to reduce human inputs and to increase the capital intensity of many operations. Computers and computer controlled machinery are beginning to find a place in the Mexican factory, although the introduction of robot technology has been slow.

The Mexican textile and apparel industry faces stiff competition from international competitors in the development of export markets. Much of Mexico's competitive advantage has been built on low wage rates, an advantage that is being undercut by very low cost producers, such as apparel firms in China. Mexico's textile sector already has some potential to compete successfully, with the apparel sector facing greater foreign competition. The textile sector needs to implement newer technology and machinery, particularly in the dyeing and finishing sectors, where bottlenecks currently reduce the ability to produce in sufficient quantities to supply potential markets. On the other hand, worker training and implementation of generic technology will be more important for the apparel sector. The industry currently has limited linkages dedicated to support of academic research or to acquisition of appropriate foreign technology. With the diverse locations of textile and apparel production, this industry may be well served by efforts to decentralize science and technology programs away from Mexico City. Further, cooperative action by the smaller producers will serve to increase interest by the Mexican government in supporting technology development for the apparel sector. In the end, a comprehensive strategy for increased technological capacity may well serve to provide a competitive edge to this sector.

The Mexican petrochemical and plastics industry continues to restructure and privatize, although it continues to be dominated by Pemex. As the plastics segment begins to fully exploit competitive advantages, it will need to modernize production technology for commodity plastic materials before seeking to create production for specialty materials. This will enable the Mexican plastics firms to serve the rapidly growing consumer market, especially in the area of product packaging. Research and development efforts will need to be focused on those areas that will provide for sufficient supply of domestic markets, such as the development of improved reactor and catalyst systems for commodity polymers. It is exactly in these areas that industry - academia cooperation will be most effective. In addition, policies will need to be implemented which provide for a consistent supply of raw materials into the sector. Current shortages of quality raw materials make production planning difficult. It is quite likely that the plastics sector, in general, will become more competitive as Pemex's dominant role extending from oil exploration to downstream plastics production is relaxed. The plastics sector is positioned to take a leading role in the transition toward improved competitiveness.

The Mexican steel industry has changed rapidly over the past decade, with the industry now effectively privatized and enjoying a renewed international competitiveness. Mexican firms are exporting significant amounts of steel, particularly to the U.S. market, and are joining with international partners in several joint ventures for technology and production. The focus on implementation of minimill technology has reduced transportation costs and increased production flexibility, giving the Mexican firms a competitive edge over U.S. integrated mills. The continued drive to invest in new technology bodes well for the future of the Mexican steel industry, as does the potential for use of scrap steel in the minimill production facilities. The high usage rate of direct reduced iron in Mexican mills makes it increasingly likely that both low value-added and high quality steel will continue to be produced at globally competitive prices.

The Mexican automobile sector has changed from a supplier of low quality cars for domestic use to a high quality exporter. In doing so, the quality of domestic vehicles has also improved. It appears to be the single most important sector for the possible creation of backward linkages to smaller firms in Mexico, and a likely pole for growth of support industries. These linkages are clearly available through the implementation of generic technology and methods, such as CAD/CAM and just-in-time inventory control. With the largest producers under foreign ownership, the industry enjoys the importation of relatively modern technology and training methods without large financial outlays by the Mexican operations. Joint ventures in the production of automobile components and automobiles are also providing newer technology and opportunities to supply U.S. production operations. For example, the Ford Hermosillo plant is quite competitive with other automobile manufacturing plants around the world. Mexico is in an excellent position to continue to grow as a supplier of vehicles and parts to both the domestic and the U.S. market.

The strategies employed by each of the distinct industrial sectors must be tailored to industry realities and needs. The textile and apparel sector, owing to the small size of the firms, needs to act collectively to import generic technology and to provide training programs. Apparel firms, in particular, need to take advantage of the decentralization of science and technology as offered through CONACYT and Mexico's higher education system. The plastics industry will need to look toward joint ventures and licensing agreements to acquire the production technologies developed in other countries. The plastics sector will need to become independently competitive, cutting its ties to providing government revenue through Pemex. The steel industry enjoys a strong position in current technology, especially in the production and use of direct reduced iron. It is therefore likely to enjoy benefits from both internal research and development and the use of cooperative technology agreements with foreign firms. The vigor of the privatized firms will continue to grow with the enhanced focus on international technology and marketing alliances. The auto industry will continue to import technology from the parents, and can act as a leader in the creation of technology and production linkages to the smaller supplier firms. The auto industry is the a strong proponent of training and education of workers, a trend which will hopefully create more interest in improving worker skills in several sectors. Most importantly, each of the sectors can create dynamic gains through the sharing of technology between firms, government, and academia.

Mexico, as a result of geographic proximity to the United States, enjoys the benefits of a large potential export market but also the threat of a very large competitor. Although past technology programs under the import substitution industrialization plan retarded the development of technological capacity, the future for Mexican industry appears to be increasingly more promising. Substantial changes in the government, academic, and industrial support for adoption of new technology are taking place. Industrial spending for acquisition and development of technology are beginning to rise, albeit from very low starting levels. This spending, coupled with the creation of new technology linkages, promises to raise the national technological capacity rapidly. Despite the recent recession, plans for capital investment and training programs continue to be implemented. Increased spending for technology transfer, as well as domestic research and development programs, bode well for aiding the ability of Mexican firms to adapt to technological and market changes. Perhaps most importantly, managers and firms in Mexico are developing a culture which embraces new technology as a tool toward increased industrial competitiveness.

---

[1] This chapter is based in part on Thomas J. Botzman, Alliances for Technology Transfer in Mexico, *American Society for Competitiveness*, Annual Research Volume, 1996.

Selected References

Aboites, J. (1994) Evolución Reciente de la Política Científica y Tecnológica de México. *Comercio Exterior*, 44(9).

Acs, Z. J. (1988) Innovation and Technical Change in the U.S. Steel Industry. *Technovation*, 181 - 195.

Aguilar Barajas, I. (1995) Las empresas micro, pequeñas y medianas en el desarrollo industrial de México. *Comercio Exterior*, 45(6).

Alarcon, D. and T. McKinley. (1997) The Rising Contribution of Labor Income to Inequality in Mexico. *North American Journal of Economics and Finance*, 8(2).

Alcántara Santuario, A. (1994) Reforma Universitaria y el Papel de las Universidades Públicas en el Desarrollo Científico y Tecnológico: El Caso de la UNAM. *Acta Sociologica*, 139-183.

Altos Hornos de Mexico. (1993) *Gestiones Contra Importaciones Desleales*. Author.

Alvarez Padilla, A. (1994) La revolución de los servicios y su impacto en el mercado informático. In Leonel Corona T., (ed.), *Empresas Innovadoras en Mexico - Economía Informa*, 34 - 40.

Amador, G.   (1996) La industria química tuvo el menor déficit comercial en cinco años. *El Economista*, 36. February 26, 1996.

American Iron and Steel Institute (AISI). (1993) *Annual Report 1992*. Washington, DC: Author.

Anderson, K. L.   (1995) Aggressively Ambitious Nucor on the War Path. *ACERO - North American Steel Journal*, 14- 19.

Anderson, S. K.   (1993) *Total Factor Productivity in Mexican Manufacturing: An Analysis of the Sources of Growth, 1975 - 1985*. (Doctoral dissertation, Texas A&M University, 1993).

Aréchiga, H. (1994) La Ciencia Mexicana en el Contexto Global.   In M. A. Porrúa (ed.), *Mexico: Ciencia y Tecnología en el Umbral del Siglo XXI*. Mexico City: Consejo Nacional de Ciencia y Tecnologia (CONACYT).

Arndt, S. W. (1991) Adjustment in the Process of Trade Liberalization: The U.S. and Mexico. *The North American Review of Economics and Finance*, 2(2), 157-165.

Asociación Nacional de la Industria Química (1995) *Anuario Estadístico de la Industria Química Mexicana*. Mexico City: Author.

Auty, R. M.   (1994) Industrial Policy Reform in Six Large Newly Industrializing Countries: The Resource Curse Thesis. *World Development* 22(1).

Banamex, Department of Economic Studies. (1993). *Monthly Bulletin - Plastics*. Mexico City: Author.

Banco Nacional de Comercio Exterior (BANCOMEXT). (1994) *Industria Química, Farmacéutica, Hule y Plasticos*. Mexico City: Author.

Banco Nacional de Comercio Exterior (BANCOMEXT). (1994) *Tratado de Libre Comercio de América del Norte, Manufacturas de Materias Plásticas*. Mexico City: Author.

Bannister, G. J., H. J. Muller, and R. R. Rehder. (1996) Ford-Mazda's Hermosillo Assembly Plant: A Quality Benchmark Cross-Cultural Alliance. *Competitive Intelligence Review*, 7(2).

Barros Valero, J. (1994) La Investigación en las Universidades Públicas de los Estados. In M. A. Porrúa (ed.), *Mexico: Ciencia y Tecnología en el Umbral del Siglo XXI.* Mexico City: Consejo Nacional de Ciencia y Tecnologia (CONACYT).

Blum, R. S. (1998) Investment Strategies and "Leaner" Production in the North American Auto Industry. In H. Juárez Núñez and S. Babson (eds.). *Confronting Change: Auto Labor and Lean Production in North America.* Puebla, Puebla: Benemérita Universidad Autónoma de Puebla.

Botella, O. C., E. García C., and J. Giral B. (1991) Textiles: Mexican Perspective. In Sidney Weintraub, Luis Rubio F., and Alan D. Jones (Eds.), *U.S. - Mexican Industrial Integration: The Road to Free Trade.* Boulder, Colorado: Westview Press.

Botzman, T. J. (1996) Alliances for Technology Transfer in Mexico. *Journal of Global Competitiveness*, 4(1).

Botzman, T. J., W. Howell, and M. P. Tello. (1996) American Managerial Strategies for Retaining Personnel and Applications to Mexico. *Midwest Review of International Business Research.*

Botzman, T. J., A. Elizondo, and A. Lopez. (1992) Free Trade and Changes in the North American Higher Education System, *Proceedings of the Sixth Hispanic Symposium on Business and the Economy.*

Botzman, T J. (1991) *The Impact of the U.S.-Canada Free Trade Agreement on Trade in Steel Mill Products Between the United States and Canada.* (Doctoral dissertation, Kent State University, 1991).

Botzman, T J. (1997) Prospects for Trade in the North American Steel Industry. *Ciencia ergo sum,* 4(1). Universidad Autonoma del Estado de Mexico.

Botzman, T.J. (1998) Technology and Competitiveness: A Comparison of the Mexican and US Textile and Apparel Industries. *Annual Research Volume - American Society for Competitiveness.*

Botzman, T.J. (1997) Technology and Trade in the Mexican Thermoplastic Industry. *The Anahuac Journal.*, 1(1).

Brown, D. K. (1992) The Impact of a North American Free Trade Area: Applied General Equilibrium Models. In Lustig, Nora, Barry P. Bosworth, and Robert Z. Lawrence, (Eds.), *North American Free Trade: Assessing the Impact.* Washington, DC: The Brookings Institution.

Bucay F., B. (1991) Petrochemicals: Mexican Perspective. In Sidney Weintraub, Luis Rubio F., and Alan D. Jones (Eds.), *U.S. - Mexican Industrial Integration: The Road to Free Trade.* Boulder, Colorado: Westview Press.

Bruner, E. (1998) Columbus, Ga., Textile Business Appears to be Growing with Help of NAFTA. *Columbus Ledger-Enquirer.* March 1, 1998.

Burnham, J. B. (1993) *Changes and Challenges: The Transformation of the U.S. Steel Industry.* Washington, DC: Center for the Study of American Business.

Cabrera, G. (1995) Few Mexican Homes Recycle. *ACERO - North American Steel Journal*, 12 - 15.

Cabrera, G. (1995) HYLSA Digests Its Enormous Investments. *ACERO - North American Steel Journal*, 13 - 17.

Cabrera, G. (1995) Mexican Steel Sector Strategies During the Crisis. *ACERO - North American Steel Journal*, 26 - 27.

Camacho Vargas, A. (1994) El sistema de propiedad industrial en México in Corona T., Leonel, (Ed.), *Empresas Innovadoras en Mexico - Economía Informa.*, 20 - 27.

Camara Minea de Mexico. (1993) *LVI Asamblea General Ordinaria 1993.* Mexico City: Author.

Camara Nacional de la Industria del Hierro y del Acero. (1994) *Diez Años de Estadistica Siderurgica.* Mexico City: Author.

Carlsson, B. (1994) Technological Systems and Economic Performance. In Dodgson, Mark. and Roy Rothwell, (Eds.), *The Handbook of Industrial Innovation.* Hants, England: Edward Elgar Publishing.

Castañeda, J. A., and J. A. Toledo Barraza. (1994) Propiedad Industrial e Innovación Tecnológica. In M. A. Porrúa (ed.), *Mexico: Ciencia y Tecnología en el Umbral del Siglo XXI.* Mexico City: Consejo Nacional de Ciencia y Tecnologia.

Clavijo, F., and J. I. Casar, eds. (1994) *La industria mexicana en el mercado mundial: Elementos para una politica industrial.* Fondo de Cultura Economica (FONECA).

Clavijo, F., and A. Márquez. (1994) Incentivos Públicos para la Innovación y Difusión de la Tecnología en México. In M. A. Porrúa (ed.), *Mexico: Ciencia y Tecnología en el Umbral del Siglo XXI.* Mexico City: Consejo Nacional de Ciencia y Tecnologia (CONACYT).

Cline, W. R. (1990) *The Future of World Trade in Textiles and Apparel.* Washington, DC: Institute for International Economics.

Contractor, F. J. (1986) International Business: An Alternative View. *International Marketing Review*, 21, 74 - 85.

Cooke, P., and Morgan, K. (1994) The Creative Milieu: A Regional Perspective on Innovation. In M. Dodgson and R. Rothwell (Eds.), *The Handbook of Industrial Innovation.* Hants, England: Edward Elgar Publishing.

Corona Treviño, L. (1994) Hacia la consolidación de las empresas innovadoras. *Economía Informa*, 6 - 13.

Corona Treviño, L. (1994) Las experiencias en los procesos de innovación. *Economía Informa*, 4 - 5.

Correa, C. M. (1994) El Nuevo Escenario para la Transferencia de Tecnología: Repercusiones en los Países en Desarrollo. *Comercio Exterior*, 44(9).

Cortelesse, C. (1993) Competitividad de los Sistemas Productivos y las Empresas Pequeñas y Medianas: Campo para la Cooperación Internacional, *Comercio Exterior*, 43(6).

Crandall, R. W. (1987) A Sectoral Perspective: Steel. In Robert M. Stern, Philip H. Trezise, and John Whalley (Eds.), *Perspectives on a U.S.-Canadian Free Trade Agreement.* Washington, DC: The Brookings Institution, 231 - 243.

Crandall, R. W. (1993) *Manufacturing on the Move.* Washington, DC: The Brookings Institution.

Crandall, R. W. (1981) *The U.S. Steel Industry in Recurrent Crisis: Policy Options in a Competitive World.* Washington, DC: The Brookings Institution.

Daly, Donald J. (1991) International Competitiveness of Japanese Manufacturing. *Managerial and Decision Economics*, 12.

Daly, Donald J. (1993) Porter's Diamond and Exchange Rates. *Management International Review*, 33(2).

de Maria y Campos, M. (1993) Hacia un Desarrollo de las Micro y Pequeñas Industrias Compatible con el Cuidado del Ambiente. *Comercio Exterior*, 43(6).

Dean, C. C., and J. Le Master. (1991) Present Barriers to Technology Transfer: U.S. to Eastern Europe Versus U.S. to Mexico. *The International Executive*, 33(3).

Deily, M. E. (1991) Exit Strategies and Plant-Closing Decisions: The Case of Steel. *Rand Journal of Economics,* 22(2), 250 - 263.

Dodgson, M. and R. Rothwell, Eds. (1994) *The Handbook of Industrial Innovation.* Hants, England: Edward Elgar Publishing.

Dosi, G. (1988) Sources, Procedures, and Microeconomic Effects of Innovation. *Journal of Economic Literature,* 26(3).

Drucker, P.F. (1990) The Emerging Theory of Manufacturing. *Harvard Business Review,* 68(3).

Dunning, J. (1993) *Multinational Enterprises and the Global Economy.* Reading, Massachusetts: Addison-Wesley Publishing Company.

Dussel Peters, E. (1995) El cambio estructural del sector manufacturero Mexicano, 1988 - 1994, *Comercio Exterior,* 45(6).

Ebel, K. H. (1991) Computer-integrated manufacturing: A new menace for developing countries. *International Labour Review,* 130 (5-6).

Erceg, C. J., P. R. Israelivich, and R. H. Schnorbus. (1989) Competitive Pricing Behavior in the U.S. Steel Industry. *Economic Perspectives,* 13(2).

Espinosa, J., ed. (1993) *The Statistical Guide to the Metals Industries: Metal Statistics 1993.* New York: American Metal Market, Chilton Publications.

Export efforts begin to pay off for US firms. (1997) *Textile World,* 147(6), 97.

Fagerberg, J. (1994) Technology and International Differences in Growth Rates. *Journal of Economic Literature,* 32.

Fenton, F. (1995) The Multilateral Steel Agreement: What's Holding It Up? *ACERO - North American Steel Journal,* 26 - 27.

Ferris, D. (1996) Mexico Beckons. *Ward's Auto World,* 32(7).

Folkerts-Landau, D. and T. Ito. (1995) *International Capital Markets: Developments, Prospects, and Policy Issues.* Washington, DC: International Monetary Fund.

Fonseca, J. C. (1995) IMSA's Santiago Clariond: It's Imperative to Maintain Technological Investment. *ACERO - North American Steel Journal,* 32 - 33.

Ford, T.   (1995) Packaging market faces numerous hurdles.   *Plastics News*, 19.

Fransman, M.   (1994) The Japanese Innovation System: How Does It Work? in Dodgson, Mark. and Roy Rothwell, eds.   *The Handbook of Industrial Innovation*. Hants, England: Edward Elgar Publishing.

Ganado, A. S. (1995) Panorama de la Industria del Plastico. *Comercio Exterior,* 45, 367 - 371.

García G., A., and A. Lara R.   (1998) Cambio Tecnológico y Aprendizaje Laboral en G.M.: Los casos del D.F. y Silao. In H. Juárez Núñez and S. Babson (eds.). *Confronting Change: Auto Labor and Lean Production in North America*. Puebla, Puebla: Benemérita Universidad Autónoma de Puebla.

Garcia, P. R., and S. Hills. (1998) Meeting "Lean" Competitors: Ford de México's Industrial Relations Strategy. In H. Juárez Núñez and S. Babson (eds.). *Confronting Change: Auto Labor and Lean Production in North America*.   Puebla, Puebla: Benemérita Universidad Autónoma de Puebla.

Gherson, G. (1993) Prescription for Canada's Big Steel: Bankruptcy. *Financial Times of Canada*. (April 10, 1993): 1, 4.

Golden, J. R.   (1994)   *Economics and National Strategy in the Information Age: Global Networks, Technology Policy, and Cooperative Competition*. Westport, Connecticut: Praeger.

Graham, E. M., and P. R. Krugman. (1995) *Foreign Direct Investment in the United States*. Third Edition.   Washington, DC: Institute for International Economics.

Graves, A. (1994) Innovation in a Globalizing Industry: The Case of Automobiles. in Dodgson, Mark. and Roy Rothwell, eds. *The Handbook of Industrial Innovation*. Hants, England: Edward Elgar Publishing, 1994.

Greene, A. P. (1994) Perspectivas de una Politica Tecnologíca: Hacia la Construcción de un Sistema Nacional de Innovación. In M. A. Porrúa (ed.), *Mexico: Ciencia y Tecnología en el Umbral del Siglo XXI.* Mexico City: Consejo Nacional de Ciencia y Tecnologia (CONACYT).

Gruber, W., D. Mehta, and R. Vernon. (1967) The R&D Factor in International Trade and International Investment of United States Industries. *Journal of Political Economy.*

Grunwald, J. (1991) Opportunity Missed: Mexico and Maquiladoras *The Brookings Review,* 9(1).

Grunwald, J. and K. Flamm. (1985) *The Global Factory: Foreign Assembly in International Trade.* Washington, DC: The Brookings Institution.

Gunther, J. W., R. R. Moore, and G. D. Short. (1996) Mexican Banks and the 1994 Peso Crisis: The Importance of Initial Conditions. *North American Journal of Economics & Finance,* 7(2).

Gutiérrez Camposeco, V. (1994) Modernización Tecnológica en la Micro, Pequeña y Mediana Empresas. In M. A. Porrúa (ed.), *Mexico: Ciencia y Tecnología en el Umbral del Siglo XXI.* Mexico City: Consejo Nacional de Ciencia y Tecnologia (CONACYT).

Hagedoorn, J. and Narula, R. (1994) Choosing Organizational Modes of Strategic Technology Partnering: International and Sectoral Differences. *Journal of International Business Studies,* 27(2), 265 - 284.

Haigh, R. W. (1992) Building a Strategic Alliance: The Hermosillo Experience as a Ford-Mazda Proving Ground. *Columbia Journal of World Business.*

Herrera, Alicia. (1995) *Mexico - Textiles for Apparel - ISA9510.* United States Embassy, Mexico. Document 9225.

Herrera, A. (1993) *The Industrial Training Services Market in Mexico.* ISA9312. Mexico City: American Embassy.

Hirschman. A. O. (1958) *The Strategy of Economic Development.* New Haven, Connecticut: Yale University Press.

Hedges, R. M. (1993) Porter's diamond framework in a Mexican context. *Management International Review,* 33 (2), 41 - 54.

Huskonen, W. D. (1995) The New Look at Hylsa. *33 Metal Producing,* 27 - 32.

Instituto Mexicano del Plastico Industrial, S.C. (IMP).   (1995) *Situacion de la Industria del Plastico 1995 - 2000.* Mexico City: Author.

Instituto Nacional de Estadistica, Geografica e Informatica (INEGI). (1995) *La Industria Automotriz en Mexico.* Mexico City, Author.

Instituto Nacional de Estadistica, Geografica e Informatica (INEGI). (1995) *La Industria Siderurgica en Mexico.* Mexico City, Author.

Instituto Nacional de Estadistica, Geografica e Informatica (INEGI). (1995) *La Industria Textil y del Vestido en Mexico.* Mexico City, Author.

Instituto Nacional de Estadistica, Geografica e Informatica (INEGI). (1995) *XIV Censo Industrial, Industrias Manufactureras Productos y Materias Primas: Subsector 35. Sustancias quimicas, productos derivados del petroleo y del carbon, de hule y de plastico.* Mexico City, Author.

Isenberg-O'Loughlin, J. (1996) EAF Metallics: At Long Last, A Mother Lode. *33 Metal Producing,* 38 - 45.

Isenberg-O'Loughlin, J. (1996) Gallatin Enters the Thin-Slab Sweepstakes. *33 Metal Producing,* 33 - 38, 83.

Juárez Núñez, H. (1998) La Productividad y el Trabajo en el Contexto de la Producción Esbelta en VW de México. In H. Juárez Núñez and S. Babson (eds.). *Confronting Change: Auto Labor and Lean Production in North America.* Puebla, Puebla: Benemérita Universidad Autónoma de Puebla.

Juárez Núñez, H., and S. Babson. (1998) *Confronting Change: Auto Labor and Lean Production in North America.* Puebla, Puebla: Benemérita Universidad Autónoma de Puebla.

Katz, I. (1996) Exportaciones y crecimiento económico: Evidencia para la industria manufacturera en México. *Comercio Exterior*, 46(2).

Klein, J.A. (1989) The Human Costs of Manufacturing Reform. *Harvard Business Review*, 42 (2).

Koen, A.D. (1995) Slower demand growth lies ahead for U.S. petrochemical producers. *Oil & Gas Journal*, 93(26), 16 - 19.

Kokko, A. (1994) Technology, Market Characteristics, and Spillovers. *Journal of Development Economics*, 43(2), 279-293.

Kolland, F. (1990) National Cultures and Technology Transfer: The Influence of the Mexican Life Style on Technology Adaptation, *International Journal of Intercultural Relations*, 14, 319-336.

Kopinak, K. (1995) Technology and the Organization of Work in Mexican Transport Equipment Maquilas, *Studies in Political Economy*, 48, 31 - 70.

Kuster, T. (1995). U.S. mills jump on board to export. *Iron Age New Steel*, 11(9), 18 - 22.

Lall, S. (1992) Technological Capabilities and Industrialization. *World Development*. 20(2).

Lande, S. L. (1991) Textiles: United States Perspective. In Sidney Weintraub, Luis Rubio F., and Alan D. Jones (Eds.), *U.S. - Mexican Industrial Integration: The Road to Free Trade.* Boulder, Colorado: Westview Press.

Layne, D. (1993) Politicas Financieras para el Desarollo de la Pequeña Empresa. *Comercio Exterior*, 43(6).

Lazaroff, L. (1993) Grupo Alfa Charts a New Course. *El Financiero International*. Mexico City, June 21-27, 1993.

Leamer, E. (1993) U.S. Manufacturing and an Emerging Mexico. *The North American Review of Economics and Finance*, 4(1), 51-89.

Lim, L., and Fong, P. (1982) Vertical Linkages and Multinational Enterprises in Developing Countries. *World Development*, 10(7), 585 - 595.

López-de-Silanes, F. (1991) Automobiles: Mexican Perspective. In Sidney Weintraub, Luis Rubio F., and Alan D. Jones (Eds.), *U.S. - Mexican Industrial Integration: The Road to Free Trade*. Boulder, Colorado: Westview Press.

Lorey, D. E., (1996) Education and the Challenges of Mexican Development. in Randall, ed., *Changing Structure of Mexico: Political, Social, and Economic Prospects*. Armonk, New York: M. E. Sharpe.

Lowenthal, A. F. (1993) Latin America: Ready for Partnership? *Foreign Affairs*, 72(1).

Lustig, N., B. P. Bosworth, and R. Z. Lawrence, eds. (1992) *North American Free Trade: Assessing the Impact*. Washington, DC: The Brookings Institution.

Maartens, M. E. (1991) Automobiles: United States Perspective. In Sidney Weintraub, Luis Rubio F., and Alan D. Jones (Eds.), *U.S. - Mexican Industrial Integration: The Road to Free Trade*. Boulder, Colorado: Westview Press.

Maldonado Aguirre, S. (1995) La rama automovilística y los corredores industriales en el noroeste de México. *Comercio Exterior*, 45(6).

Manzanella, J. L. (1996) NAFTA Gains Grow in U.S.-Mexico Trade. *America's Textiles International*, 25(8).

Marceau, J. (1994) Clusters, Chains and Complexes: Three Approaches to Innovation with a Public Policy Perspective. In Dodgson, Mark. and Roy Rothwell, (Eds.), *The Handbook of Industrial Innovation*. Hants, England: Edward Elgar Publishing.

Marín, H. (1993) Un programa para la vinculacíon: enlace academia-industria. *Estrategia Industrial*, 11, 15 - 17.

Martinez, R. (1995) The North American Steel Industry. *ACERO - North American Steel Journal*, 40 - 42.

Martínez Garcia, M. (1994) El Sistema de Centros SEP - CONACYT. In M. A. Porrúa (ed.), *Mexico: Ciencia y Tecnología en el Umbral del Siglo XXI.* Mexico City: Consejo Nacional de Ciencia y Tecnologia (CONACYT).

Martuscelli, J. and G. Soberón. (1994) El Desarollo Tecnológico y las Universidades Mexicanas. In M. A. Porrúa (ed.), *Mexico: Ciencia y Tecnología en el Umbral del Siglo XXI.* Mexico City: Consejo Nacional de Ciencia y Tecnologia (CONACYT).

Mexican Foundry Goes from Dirt Floor to Ductile Iron. (1993). *Foundry Management & Technology*, 26 - 28.

Mexico mills making most of NAFTA. (1997) *Textile World* 147(12), 34.

Mexico's tariff boost will help US mills. (1997) *Textile World* 147(8), 20.

Micheli, J. (1996) Technology Policy in a Weak Market, in Randall, L., (ed.), *Changing Structure of Mexico: Political, Social, and Economic Prospects.* Armonk, New York: M. E. Sharpe.

Molina, I. (1995) Hacia un plan nacional de investigación y desarrollo. *Comercio Exterior*, 45(11).

Morris, G. (1995) Petchems Productive Push: Contrary Cycles. *Chemical Week*, S11.

Moss, J. J. (1990) The 1990 Mexican Technology Transfer Regulations. *Stanford Journal of International Law*, 27.

Murray, J. Y. (1995) Patterns in Domestic vs. International Strategic Alliances: An Investigation of U.S. Multinational Firms. *Multinational Business Review*, 3(2).

Nakata, C., and K. Sivakumar. (1996) National Culture and New Product Development: An Integrative Review. *Journal of Marketing*, 60(1).

National Research Council, National Materials Advisory Board, Commission on Engineering and Technical Systems. (1990) *Competitiveness of the U.S. Minerals and Metals Industry.* Washington, DC: National Academy Press.

National Science Board. (1996)   Technology Development and Competitiveness.   *Science and Engineering Indicators.* Chapter 6.

National Science Board. (1993)   Technology Development and Diffusion. *Science and Engineering Indicators.* Chapter 6.

O'Brien, M.   (1991) Salinastroika: Recent Developments in Technology Transfer Law in Mexico. *St. Mary's Law Journal..*

Olmedo Carranza, B.   (1996) Industrialización y sector externo en América Latina y México. *Comercio Exterior*, 46(2).

Organization for Economic Cooperation and Development (OECD). (1996) *OECD Economic Surveys: Mexico 1997.*   Paris: Author.

Organization for Economic Cooperation and Development (OECD). (1996) *Industrial Competitiveness.* Paris: Author.

Organization for Economic Cooperation and Development (OECD). (1997)   *Industrial   Competitiveness: Benchmarking Environments in the Global Economy.* Paris: Author.

Organization for Economic Cooperation and Development (OECD). (1994) *Reviews of National Science and Technology Policy: Mexico.* Paris: Author.

Organization for Economic Cooperation and Development (OECD). (1996) *Technology and Industrial Performance.*   Paris: Author.

Organization for Economic Cooperation and Development (OECD). (1996) *Trade Liberalisation Policies in Mexico.*   Paris: Author.

Ostry, S. and R. R. Nelson. (1995) *Techno-Nationalism and Techno-Globalism: Conflict and Cooperation.* Washington, DC: The Brookings Institution.

Parkinson, G. (1991) Steelmaking Renaissance. *Chemical Engineering,* 98(5).

Patel, S., (Ed.). (1993) *Technological Transformation in the Third World.* Hants, England: Avebury Publishers.

Peña Díaz, A. (1994) Los Investigadores Científicos que México Necesita. In M. A. Porrúa (ed.), *Mexico: Ciencia y Tecnología en el Umbral del Siglo XXI.* Mexico City: Consejo Nacional de Ciencia y Tecnologia (CONACYT).

Pfaff, J. F., J. Garcia Sordo, T. Schwarz, S. Trevino, C. J. Sepulveda M., and C. G. Villarreal Dominguez. (1993) Technology Transfer in Mexico: Past Patterns and New Problems Related to the North American Free Trade Agreement, *The International Executive,* 35(2).

Phillips, G. T. (1993) Las Pequeñas Empresas de Estados Unidos. *Comercio Exterior,* 43(6).

Porter, M. E. (1990) *The Competitive Advantage of Nations.* New York: The Free Press.

Porter, M. E. (1985) *Competitive Advantage: Creating and Sustaining Superior Performance.* New York: The Free Press.

Porrúa, M. A. (1994) *Mexico: Ciencia y Tecnología en el Umbral del Siglo XXI.* Mexico City: Consejo Nacional de Ciencia y Tecnologia (CONACYT).

Preston, J. (1996) With Piracy Booming in Mexico, U.S. Industry's Cries Get Louder, *The New York Times,* 145, April 20, 1996.

Quijada, R. (1991) Petrochemicals: U.S. Perspective. In S. Weintraub, L. Rubio F., and A. D. Jones (Eds.). *U.S. - Mexico Industrial Integration: The Road to Free Trade.* Boulder, Colorado: Westview Press.

Quintanilla M., J., and M. Bauer E. (1996) Mexican Oil and Energy. in L. Randall, ed., *Changing Structure of Mexico: Political, Social, and Economic Prospects.* Armonk, New York: M. E. Sharpe.

Raafat, F. (1992) Training and Technology Transfer: Efforts of Japanese, Mexican, and American Maquiladora Companies in Mexico. *Socio-Economic Planning Science*, 26, 181 - 190.

Randall, L., ed., (1996) *Changing Structure of Mexico: Political, Social, and Economic Prospects.* Armonk, New York: M. E. Sharpe.

Rodríguez-Clare, A. (1996) Multinationals, Linkages, and Economic Development. *The American Economic Review*, 86(4), 852 - 873.

Rodríguez-Clare, A. (1996) The Division of Labor and Economic Development. *Journal of Development Economics*, 49, 3 - 32.

Rothwell, R., and Dodgson, M. (1994) Innovation and Size of Firm. In M. Dodgson and R. Rothwell (Eds.), *The Handbook of Industrial Innovation.* Hants, England: Edward Elgar Publishing.

Rothwell, Roy. (1994) Industrial Innovation: Success, Strategy, Trends. In M. Dodgson and R. Rothwell (Eds.), *The Handbook of Industrial Innovation.* Hants, England: Edward Elgar Publishing.

Rubio, R. (1984) *Technology Transfer and the Comparative Performance of Business Enterprises: The Case of Mexico* (Doctoral dissertation, Cornell University, 1984).

Rudomín, P. (1994) Algunas Reflexiones Acerca del Sistema Nacional de Investigadores. In M. A. Porrúa (ed.), *Mexico: Ciencia y Tecnología en el Umbral del Siglo XXI.* Mexico City: Consejo Nacional de Ciencia y Tecnologia (CONACYT).

Ruiz Durán, C. (1993) México: Crecimiento e Innovación en las Micro y Pequeñas Empresas. *Comercio Exterior*, 43(6).

Russell, J. M. (1995) The Increasing Role of International Cooperation in Science and Technology Research in Mexico. *Scientometrics*, 33(1).

Salinas Chavez, A. (1992) Hacia la competitividad e internacionalización de la industria textile. *Comercio Exterior*, 42(9), 822-828.

Samways, N. L. (1994) Developments in the North American Iron and Steel Industry. *Iron and Steel Engineer* 2 : D-1 to D-20.

Sánchez Ugarte, F. (1993) Acciones en Favor de las Micro, Pequeñas y Medianas Empresas en México. *Comercio Exterior*, 43(6).

Sánchez Ugarte, F. (1994) La Modernización Tecnológica de la Industria Mexicana. In M. A. Porrúa (ed.), *Mexico: Ciencia y Tecnología en el Umbral del Siglo XXI.* Mexico City: Consejo Nacional de Ciencia y Tecnologia (CONACYT).

Sargent, J. and L. Matthews. (1997) Skill Development and Integrated Manufacturing in Mexico. *World Development,* 25 (10).

Scherrer, C. (1988) Mini-Mills a New Growth Path for the U.S. Steel Industry. *Journal of Economic Issues,* 22(4), 1179 - 1200.

Scheuerman, W. E. (1990) Joint Ventures in the U.S. Steel Industry: Steel's Restructuring Attempts to Achieve Tighter Control Over Raw Material Markets. *American Journal of Economics and Sociology*, 49(4), 413 - 429.

Schmidt, B. (1995) A New International Stance. *ACERO - North American Steel Journal,* 10 - 14.

Secretaria de Comercio y Fomento Industrial (SECOFI), Direccion General de Politica Industrial. (1995) *Diagnostico del Sector de Plasticos.* Mexico City: Author.

Secretaría del Trabajo y Previsión Social (STPS) and Instituto Nacional de Estadística, Geografía e Informática (INEGI). (1995) *Encuesta Nacional de Empleo Salarios Tecnologica y Capacitation en el Sector Manufacturero 1992.* Mexico City: Authors.

Sagafi-nejad, T.   (1991) International Technology Transfer Literature: Advances in Theory, Empirical Research, and Policy. In R. D. Robinson (Ed.),   *The International Communication of Technology: A Book of Readings.*   New York: Taylor & Francis.

Sagafi-nejad, T.   (1995) Transnational Corporations - Host Country Relations and the Changing Foreign Direct Investment Climate: Toward 2000. *The International Trade Journal*, 9(1).

Shaiken, H.   (1994) Advanced Manufacturing and Mexico: A New International Division of Labor? *Latin American Research Review,* 29(2), 39 - 71.

Shaiken, H.   (1991) The Universal Motors Assembly and Stamping Plant: Transferring High-Tech Production to Mexico. *Columbia Journal of World Business,* 26(2).

Sharp, M.   (1994) Innovation in the Chemicals Industry. In M. Dodgson and R. Rothwell (Eds.),   *The Handbook of Industrial Innovation.*   Hants, England: Edward Elgar Publishing.

Siggel, E.   (1996) Trade policy reform and industrial sector growth in Mexico: 1960 - 1991. *Canadian Journal of Economics, 29.*

Sklair, L.   (1993) *Assembling for development: the maquila industry in Mexico and the United States.*   San Diego: Center for U.S.- Mexican Studies, University of California - San Diego.

Sobarzo, H. E. (1992) A General Equilibrium Analysis of the Gains From Trade for the Mexican Economy of a NAFTA. *The World Economy*, 15, 83 - 100.

Sterner, T. (1990) Ownership, Technology, and Efficiency: An Empirical Study of Cooperatives, Multinationals, and Domestic Enterprises in the Mexican Cement Industry. *Journal of Comparative Economics*, 14, 286 - 300.

Studer, M. I.   (1998) Regionalism in the Ford Motor Company's Global Strategies. In H. Juárez Núñez and S. Babson (eds.). *Confronting Change: Auto Labor and Lean Production in North America.*   Puebla, Puebla: Benemérita Universidad Autónoma de Puebla.

Sutter, M. (1997) Material Gains: Mexican textile industry is healthy and has a bright future in terms of growth. *Business Mexico,* 7(9).

Szekely, J. (1995) Whither Mini-Mills? *33 Metal Producing,* 57-59, 90.

Teece, D. J. (1991) Innovation, Trade, and Economic Welfare: Contrasts Between Petrochemicals and Semiconductors. *The North American Review of Economics and Finance* 2(2).

Terrones López, V. (1993) Las Micro, Pequeñas y Medianas Empresas en el Proceso de Globalización. *Comercio Exterior,* 43(6).

Thurston, C. W. (1995) Outlook: The Americas '95 - Mexican Slowdown. *Chemical Marketing Reporter* 248(10), SR 10.

Tilton, J. E., ed. (1990) *World Metal Demand: Trends and Prospects.* Washington, DC: Resources for the Future.

Truett, D. B., and L. J. Truett. (1994) Technology and Input Demand: The Case of Mexican Steel Scrap Imports. *North American Journal of Economics & Finance,* 5(1), 99 - 110.

Unger, K. (1991) The Automotive Industry: Technological Change and Sourcing from Mexico. *North American Journal of Economics & Finance,* 2(2),109 - 128.

United Nations Centre on Transnational Corporations (UNCTC). (1992) *Foreign Direct Investment and Industrial Restructuring in Mexico: Government policy, corporate strategies and regional integration.* (Series A, No. 18). New York: Author.

United Nations Development Programme (UNDP). (1997) *Human Development Report.* New York: Author.

U.S. Congress. Congressional Budget Office. (1984) *The Effect of Import Quotas on the Steel Industry,* by Louis L. Schorsch. Washington, DC: Government Printing Office.

United States Department of Commerce. Bureau of the Census. (1990 - 1998, Various Issues) *U.S. Exports of Merchandise.*

United States Department of Commerce. Bureau of the Census. (1990 - 1999, Various Issues) *U.S. Imports of Merchandise.*

United States. House. Committee on Government Operations. Commerce, Consumer, and Monetary Affairs Subcommittee. (1993) *The North American Free Trade Agreement (NAFTA) and its impact on the textile/apparel/fiber and auto and auto parts industries: hearing,* May 4, 1993.

United States House of Representatives. Committee on Science, Space, and Technology; Subcommittee on Science. (1992) *Latin American Scientific Cooperation,* Tuesday, March 17, 1992.

Vernon, R. (1966) International Investment and International Trade in the Product Cycle. *Quarterly Journal of Economics.*

Vicario, M.E., and J. Steinberg. (1997) A Discussion Paper Based on the Report: North American Labor Markets - A Comparative Profile. *North American Journal of Economics & Finance,* 8(2).

Villalvazo Naranjo, J. (1994) Las incubadoras de empresas y los mecanismos de vinculación. *Economía Informa,* 14 - 19.

Villavicencio, D. (1994) Las Pequeñas y Medianas Empresas Innovadoras. *Comercio Exterior,* 44(9).

Warner, M. (1994) Innovation and Training. In M. Dodgson and R. Rothwell (Eds.), *The Handbook of Industrial Innovation.* Hants, England: Edward Elgar Publishing.

Warning on Asian Textiles. (1998) *Mexico Business Monthly,* 8(4), 12.

Weintraub, S. (1990) *A Marriage of Convenience: Relations Between Mexico and the United States.* New York: Oxford University Press.

Weintraub, S. (1992) Modeling the Industrial Effects of NAFTA in Lustig, N., B. P. Bosworth, and R. Z. Lawrence, (Eds.) *North*

American Free Trade: Assessing the Impact. Washington, DC: The Brookings Institution.

Weintraub, S., L. Rubio F., and A. D. Jones, (Eds.), (1991) *U.S. - Mexican Industrial Integration: The Road to Free Trade.* Boulder, Colorado: Westview Press.

Weisskoff, R. and E. Wolff. (1977) Linkages and Leakages: Industrial Tracking in an Enclave Economy. *Economic Development and Cultural Change,* 25(4).

Whipp, R. (1997) Direct Reduction Comes of Age. *33 Metal Producing.* May.

Whiting, V. R. (1991) Mexico's New Liberalism in Foreign Investment and Technology: Policy Choice and Global Structure. *Columbia Journal of World Business,* 26(2).

Williams, H. R. and T. J. Botzman. (1994) The U.S.-Canada Free Trade Agreement: Impact on the U.S. Steel Industry. *The American Economist,* 28(1).

Wilson, P. A. (1992) *Exports and Local Development: Mexico's New Maquiladoras.* Austin, Texas: University of Texas Press.

World Bank (1998) *World Development Report.* New York: Oxford University Press.

Wylie, P. J. (1995) Partial Equilibrium Estimates of Manufacturing Trade Creation and Diversion Due to NAFTA. *The North American Review of Economics and Finance,* 6(1), 65 - 84.

Zelade, R. (1996) About Face: Mexico's Steel Industry. *International Business,* 29 - 30.